MENUS
AND MUSIC

SHARON O'CONNOR'S

VOLUME II

MENUS AND MUSIC

BEFORE DINNER

A COOKBOOK OF
HORS D'OEUVRES
WITH A MUSICAL
CASSETTE FOR THE
COCKTAIL HOUR

Menus and Music Productions, Inc.
Piedmont, California

Library of Congress Cataloging in Publication Data
O'Connor, Sharon. 1948–
Menus and Music™
Before Dinner
A Cookbook of Hors d'Oeuvres with a Musical Cassette
for the Cocktail Hour
Music by Cole Porter, George Gershwin, Duke Ellington

Includes index
1. Cookery   2. Entertaining
I. Title
86-61766
ISBN 0-9615150-1-5 (pbk.)

Menus and Music is published by

Menus and Music Productions, Inc.
48 Inverleith Terrace
Piedmont, CA 94611
(415) 482-4800 or 845-6614

Book and Cover Design by Sharon Smith Design
Cover Photograph by Jim Sadlon
Food Styling by Sharon Polster
Piano by Yamaha
Composition by Design and Type

Manufactured in the United States of America

First Printing August 1986
10 9 8 7 6 5 4 3 2

CONTENTS

ACKNOWLEDGMENTS

My affectionate thanks to Nathan Rubin, James Shallenberger, David George, Don Haas, Mario Suraci, and Tom Duckworth, fellow members of the Classic Jazz Septet. I want to especially thank Don Haas for the arrangements and his support of this project. To Phil Edwards, the engineer with ears, and also Steve Atkins at Coast Recorders, San Francisco.

My gratitude to the chefs and managers who contributed their menus and recipes to this book, and my sincere thanks to Michael Walsh for writing the foreword.

Once again thanks to my editor, Carolyn Miller, for being so flexible and thorough. To Sharon Smith for her wonderful design, advice, and generous support of this project.

Special thanks to Sharon Polster of Edible Art for the food styling, Jim Sadlon for the photograph, and Rob Schwarzenbach for the calligraphy. To Gary Luenberger for the use of the Yamaha piano which appears on the cover. To Dascha Keig for the French translation on page 14. To Eva Kreshka at Mills College, and to the audience at the Bach Dynamite and Dancing Society.

With love and thanks to John Coreris for his help with the conception and production of this project.

FOREWORD

It was just one of those things, one of those places where, suddenly, everything came together. It was a time of elegance: Fred Astaire, gaily bedecked on a Los Angeles sound stage in a top hat (and *Top Hat*), or wandering forlornly down by the docks, singing *They Can't Take That Away from Me*. It was a time of danger: the hunt for the Maltese Falcon cost Miles Archer his life on a foggy San Francisco side street. It was a time of decadence: tomatoes like Velma Valento were too hot to handle, so Philip Marlowe bid them *Farewell My Lovely*, and the satin doll Carmen Sternwood rounded off her brother-in-law's little life with *The Big Sleep*. Who knew where the next Black Dahlia might turn up? California was *hot*; night and day, it got under your skin. Raymond Chandler, who knew it well, and saw it all, wrote:

> There was a desert wind blowing that night. It was one of those hot dry Santa Anas that come down through the mountain passes and curl your hair and make your nerves jump and your skin itch. On nights like that every booze party ends in a fight. Meek little wives feel the edge of the carving knife and study their husbands' necks . . .

Less homicidal, more sophisticated ladies might consider wielding their blades in the kitchen instead, whipping up something using the fresh ingredients from the local dairy farms, or crisp produce hauled in from the Central Valley as the prelude to a kiss. America's love affair with the California lush life was beginning in earnest. George Gershwin and Duke Ellington's names are indelibly attached to New York. But even the toughest, 'A'-training New Yorkers couldn't resist Hollywood's siren song, and with each tap of

Astaire's toe, Gershwin and the other songwriters moved a little farther west in the American consciousness.

What happened in California? Up north, the snooty San Franciscans traced their lineage back two or three generations to some robber baron or claim jumper and thought they were royalty; immigrant Italians took one look at Mount Tam and thought of Vesuvius. Down south, the Okies had fled their dust bowl, transplanting their large families and their flat midwestern accents to the dusty soil where, with a little water from somewhere, they took root and flourished. The descendants of the Vikings beached their longboats and took over Solvang. The Mexicans had always been here. And everybody was hungry.

Hungry for food, hungry for culture, hungry for self-improvement. Who needed somebody to watch over them? The rest of the country had questions, California had answers; the rest of the country had problems, California had solutions. Uniquely ours, like our chow and our climate. No matter how far away a Californian is from home, there is always the memory of the heat (only an easterner would observe in wonder that it's a dry heat), the smell of the desert's dust and of the ocean's breeze, of the pine woods and the eucalyptus trees. And the food, the best in the world. They really can't take that away from us. So keep serving it up, California. Our love is here to stay.

—*Michael Walsh*

Michael Walsh grew up in Southern California. He wrote for the *San Francisco Examiner* before assuming his current position as music critic for *Time* magazine.

INTRODUCTION

Before Dinner gives you the chance to enjoy great music, food, and drinks together! It will increase your enjoyment of the cocktail hour, a tradition as distinctively American as classic American jazz. I think the two go together hand in glove, so I asked the chefs who contributed to *Before Dinner* to prepare menus and recipes that would be complemented by the music on the accompanying cassette.

The cocktail party has been a part of good living in this country since early in the century. Tastes have changed, but at its best, it still consists of a convivial group, hors d'oeuvres, drinks, and good music in the background. At the turn of the century cocktails were served in high society circles in the United States, but in other countries their consumption was not considered good form, and the custom was confined to sporting or "fast" persons. Most of the "classic" cocktail drinks were created during the 1920s and 30s in the United States, or by Americans who were living abroad. During Prohibition, people couldn't obtain legal liquor, so to disguise the terrible flavor of hooch, cocktails proliferated. Prohibition was repealed by President Roosevelt in 1933, and the Cocktail Age arrived. Giving a cocktail party was the height of fashionable entertainment. Sipping drinks and munching on small snacks was informal and friendly and replaced the earlier tradition of entertaining with pomp and servants.

As the custom of drinking cocktails spread among the social trendsetters of the world's great cities, American-style bars sprang up everywhere. There was a lack of trained bartenders outside the United States, and many American professional bartenders found a lucrative niche in Europe, such as Harry Craddock in London who made the bar at the Savoy a mecca for cocktail drinkers. Noel Coward used cocktails as a sign of sophistication in his plays *The Vortex* and *Fallen Angels*—his "bright young things" soaked them up. In the more serious world of the late 1930s, and in a reaction to the furious pleasure-seeking of the previous decade, cocktail parties went into a decline. The more sober and economical sherry party was introduced, and then came the aridity of the war years.

Today cocktail parties are back in fashion, and most of the famous drinks of the twenties and thirties are even more popular now than when they were dreamed up by barmen in New York, Paris, and London fifty years ago. But cocktail parties are not limited to mixed drinks; people are drinking more wine, champagne, beer, and sparkling water today. I once performed music for a cocktail hour where fresh orange juice was one of the featured drinks before a dinner to celebrate the eighty-fifth birthday of Dr. Linus Pauling. Wine and champagne are enjoyed because they enhance the fine food that is now an important ingredient of a cocktail party. Beer has come a long way from having ginger ale added to it, a drink popular in the thirties, and we now have a choice of excellent American beers as well as beers from around the world. Many people prefer beverages with less alcoholic content for reasons of health and safety. Sparkling waters are a good suggestion for guests not drinking alcohol. But new cocktails are still being invented, and introducing something unexpected to your bar, such as some of the drinks presented here, adds pizzazz to a party. The cocktail party is faintly wicked, pleasantly nostalgic, and remarkably enduring!

Music is an important part of a cocktail party. It instantly sets the tone of a party and brings people together like nothing else. I have performed music at social gatherings for the past ten years, and on each occasion people have come up to say that the music made the party for them. Music at a party is such a civilized extravagance, and people want to act the part by being more charming and witty, acting more like ladies and gentlemen. The San Francisco String Quartet usually performs classical and light classical music for dinner music, but during the cocktail hour we play jazz standards—this music suits the cocktail hour. The songs recorded on the cassette are some of my favorites from this repertoire. I added a jazz trio to the string quartet for this project to create the Classic Jazz Septet, and pianist Don Haas did the arrangements of these American classics. Music infuses a cocktail party with energy and heightens the tone of the whole event—it puts a party a little over the top!

Interesting and delicious hors d'oeuvres are an essential ingredient of a cocktail party. These small bites or snacks can be almost any kind of food that can be attractively prepared and easily eaten. It is better to have a few beautifully made hors d'oeuvres in sufficient quantity than to attempt too great a variety. The actual number of hors d'oeuvres you prepare depends on the number of guests, time of day, and the duration of the party. Experts tend to disagree on the formulas of how many hors d'oeuvres to prepare, so I suggest that you be generous in your estimates.

Hors d'oeuvres present a great opportunity for the home cook to try innovative recipes, since people will usually be more adventurous with a new food if they only have to try one bite of it rather than a whole course. If the group at the party is diverse, the cook can satisfy different tastes with many little dishes, some more unusual than others. This book includes recipes that can be used as a first course for a dinner party. These could be served either in the living room on small plates as guests are gathering and enjoying a drink, or at the table.

The cocktail party is one of the easiest and most versatile ways to entertain at home. Most of the following recipes are inventive but not difficult to prepare. Hors d'oeuvres can usually be prepared in advance, which allows you to be a participating host or hostess rather than spending time in the kitchen during the party. These recipes can be used as the promise of a good meal to come, for a standard two-hour cocktail party, or as a substitute for dinner at a large extended party.

American ingenuity is adapting the cocktail hour and party to suit our life style today. We have experienced a culinary revolution in America during the past ten years and a change in our drinking habits. This collection of menus and recipes certainly reflects that. The musical compositions on the cassette are traditional, but adapting them for string quartet and jazz trio together is new. This volume of *Menus and Music* will help you create the right ambience for a wonderful cocktail hour. Enjoying companionable conversation with delicious food, drinks, and great music will never go out of style. Cheers! Enjoy!

—*Sharon O'Connor*

MUSICAL MENU

COCKTAILS: Brew Beck's Beer . . . Salt Peanuts

SOUP AND SALADS: Duke Soup . . . Dizzy Gespacho . . . Porter Cole Slaw . . . Django Rheinhearts of Palm

ENTREES: Blue Monkfish . . . Pork Pie . . . Beef Ellington (in Peking, Peking Duke) . . . Drumsticks . . . Gerry Mulligan Stew . . . St. Louis Bluesfish . . . Count Basil Spaghetti Sauce . . . Trombone Steak . . . Lionel Hampton . . . Dixielamb Chops . . . Yardbird with Oregano . . . Art Pepper Steak . . . Porgy and Bouillabess . . . Chicken Fats Waller

VEGETABLES: Swing Beans . . . Artie Shaw Vinaigrette . . . French Quarter Fries . . . Zootabagas . . . Art Tatum au Gratin . . . Fried Zootchinis . . . Cornet on the Cob

BREADS, SANDWICHES, AND PASTRIES: Charlie Parker House Rolls . . . Calloway Rye Bread . . . Piano Tuna Sandwich . . . Hoagie Carmichael . . . Raisin Miles Danish . . . Jelly Roll Morton

DESSERT: Tart Blakey (with Blakey Pastry) . . . Chi-Vaughn Cake with Bluesberry Sauce . . . Blueberry Wayne Shortcake . . . Ladyfingers with Black and Tan Ices

A MUSICAL NOTE

One of the pioneer examples of chance or indeterminate music first appeared in a cookbook. Musicians such as Erik Satie, Jean Cocteau, and Darius Milhaud contributed articles to the *Almanac de Cocagne*, a cookbook published in Paris during the twenties. In Darius Milhaud's "Cocktail," a baritone sings a recipe for a drink. His accompaniment is four clarinets in different ranges that repeat patterns of notes in free-form rhythm until the recipe is concluded. The lyrics to the piece are the following cocktail recipe.

"Fill a glass three quarters full of crushed ice. Add two teaspoons of sugar syrup, a teaspoon of lemon juice, four drops of angostura bitters, a teaspoon of absinthe, and one shot-glass of gin. Moisten the rim of a glass with a slice of lemon and dust it gently with sifted powdered sugar. Shake the mixture well and pour it into the glass which you have prepared. Grate a little nutmeg over the top and add three small cherries. Serve with large straws."

NOTES ABOUT THE COMPOSERS

Cole Porter (1891–1964)
I've Got You Under My Skin, Just One of Those Things, Night and Day

Cole Porter, the man who once owned a palazzo in Venice and apartments in Paris, and who drank champagne cocktails at the Ritz and daiquiris at the Florida Bar in Havana, grew up as a farm boy in Peru, Indiana. He moved away to attend Yale University, where he took undergraduate classes to prepare himself for law school but excelled in the Glee Club, Mandolin Club, and writing the words and music for the college smokers for Delta Kappa Epsilon and the Yale Dramatic Association. He was also introduced to the "rich rich," as he called them, during college, and found that he liked their formality and extravagance and reveled in their style. On graduation he was voted the most entertaining, the second most original, and one of the most eccentric by his senior class.

After college Porter studied music in Europe briefly at the Schola Cantorum with Vincent d'Indy and then moved to Paris, where he concentrated on contemporary popular music based on new American rhythms. He wrote songs for his own amusement and for his friends, especially, as he said later, songs that would "escape the stiff four-measure pattern of the then-reigning popular song." Hallmarks of a Cole Porter song are the fitting of note lengths and stresses to the natural accents of the words, and the tailoring of the measures to the sense of the song.

Cole Porter and Linda Lee Thomas married in Paris in 1919, and for the next nine years they were part of the inner circle of international society. During this social whirl, Porter gave musical performances at the parties he frequently hosted and attended, often with his good friend, famed party-giver Elsa Maxwell. During this period he also wrote an ambitious score of music for *Within the Quota*, 1923, which triumphantly premiered at the Champs-Elysees Theatre along with Darius Milhaud's *La Creation du Monde. Within the Quota* did not repeat its success in the United States, and Porter's interest in ambitious music waned.

Cole Porter arrived back in New York in 1927, and within a year he had a successful musical, *Paris*, on Broadway and was contributing songs to films and revues. He wrote the song "Night and Day" for Fred Astaire in the musical *Gay Divorce* in 1932. The song "Just One of Those Things" was part of the score for the musical *Jubilee*, 1935. There was a Cole Porter show almost every year. In 1935 the Porters moved into a house in Hollywood that was considered fitting for a great star in the 1920s and 30s. Cole became an enthusiast of Southern California, taking what he called "sun coloring" seriously, hosting lavish parties, and writing Hollywood film scores. Oscar Levant once wisecracked: "You've got to hand it to C.P. He's a rich boy who made good." Abe Burrows, who wrote and staged the musical *Can Can*, for which Porter composed the musical score, describes Porter's method of composing as follows: "He'd do the beat, then match the lyrics to the beat, then write the tune to the lyrics."

Cole Porter left a collection of beautiful and witty songs that are recognized throughout the world. When he died, the *Times* noted that the mere mention of his songs caused one to be "flooded with the nostalgic glow of an entire era." The *Daily News* said: "Porter's death marked the end of an era which beginning in the 20s and 30s revolutionized the Broadway musical—an entertainment many authorities consider the highest native American art form. There were three major composer lyricist teams: Richard Rodgers and Lorenz Hart, Jerome Kern and Oscar Hammerstein 2d, George and Ira Gershwin, and Cole Porter who worked superlatively alone."

George Gershwin (1898–1937)
A Foggy Day, Love Is Here to Stay, Someone to Watch Over Me,
They Can't Take That Away from Me

George Gershwin began his musical career at the age of fifteen as a pianist and song plugger in Tin Pan Alley. His job at Remick's, a music-publishing firm, was wonderful on-the-job training for his future career. He saw firsthand what was involved behind the scenes in producing hit tunes, his piano technique improved immensely from playing eight to ten hours a day, and the job gave him plenty of opportunity to improvise at the piano, experimenting with new runs, chords, and modulations. After two years Gershwin left this job and sought to enter the musical comedy field. He was hired as a rehearsal pianist for a musical with a score by Victor Herbert and Jerome Kern, and he also composed a few songs that were sung in a concert by some of the stars of the show. These songs were brought to the attention of Max Dreyfus, head of T.B. Harms, probably the most important publishing company in Tin Pan Alley. Dreyfus proposed that Gershwin continue to write songs and submit them for consideration to Harms, who would pay Gershwin royalties for each song published. During this period of employment at Harms, Gershwin met Irving Berlin. Berlin brought in his "Revolutionary Rag" to see if Harms might be interested in publishing it. "George was around the office at the time, and Dreyfus called upon him to give the rag a run-through. Berlin remembers: 'He sent this kid in. I couldn't hear my own tune—but it was brilliant.' Clearly George was up to his old harmonics and plugging a number—even to its own composer!" (*The Gershwin Years*)

In 1919 Gershwin succeeded in writing a complete score for a

Broadway musical and the song that was his first smash hit, "Swanee." In the next few years he also composed a movement for string quartet and a one-act jazz opera. Gershwin wanted to expand his activities beyond Tin Pan Alley and Broadway musical comedy and into the concert hall. He was asked by Paul Whiteman in 1924 to write a work for piano and orchestra for a concert in Aeolian Hall that was billed as "An Experiment in Modern Music." A distinguished panel of musicians would judge "What Is American Music" at the Whiteman concert. For this occasion Gershwin composed and performed his most famous piece, *Rhapsody in Blue*. He conceived the piece while he was traveling by train to Boston:

> At this stage of the piece I was summoned to Boston for the premiere of *Sweet Little Devil*. I had already done some work on the rhapsody. It was on the train, with its steely rhythms, its rattle-ty bang that is often so stimulating to a composer. . . . I frequently hear music in the very heart of noise. And there I suddenly heard—and even saw on paper—the complete construction of the rhapsody, from beginning to end. No new themes came to me, but I worked on the thematic material already in mind and tried to conceive the composition as a whole. I heard it as a sort of musical kaleidoscope of America—of our vast melting pot, of our unduplicated national pep, of our blues, our metropolitan madness. By the time I reached Boston I had a definite *plot* of the piece, as distinguished from its actual substance.

Gershwin sketched out the *Rhapsody* in a two-piano version, and Ferde Grofé did the orchestration for Whiteman's musicians. The piece and performance were received in concert with tumultuous applause and Gershwin was recognized as a composer of talent whose future work would be awaited with interest. The financial rewards of *Rhapsody* exceeded his wildest dreams.

During his entire career, Gershwin kept up a hectic schedule of partygoing. He especially loved attending parties with people of style and achievement and he tended to monopolize the piano on these occasions, usually by playing his own compositions, often whole scores. George Kaufman, who was associated with Gershwin in a number of productions, once chided George: "If you play that score one more time before we open, people are going to think you're doing a revival." In the Cole Porter musical *Jubilee* a perennial hostess boasts that the great novelty of one of her most elaborate parties is that Gershwin will *not* play the piano.

Gershwin had a desire throughout his career to study with musicians of stature, but he kept this kind of musical study subordinate to his lucrative assignments for Broadway and Hollywood. Although he may have been an indifferent music student, Gershwin was a human dynamo in pursuing his music career. In 1924 he had his first hit musical, *Lady, Be Good*, with lyrics by his brother Ira, and in 1926 he composed the score to *Oh, Kay*, which included the song "Someone to Watch Over Me." During the next few years he wrote *Concerto in F, Preludes for Piano, An American in Paris*, the score for the show *Of Thee I Sing* (which won a Pulitzer Prize), and his full-scale black opera *Porgy and Bess*, which opened in New York in 1935.

In 1936 commercial theater on Broadway was struggling for survival while Hollywood was prospering. At a time when millions of Americans were unemployed, the movies were turning out films at a modest cost for a public that needed diversion from their financial woes. Films were the major entertainment industry of the 1930s, and Gershwin became interested in a movie contract. In 1936 the Gershwins moved to Hollywood to write a musical score for a Fred Astaire–Ginger Rogers movie. Among the tunes the Gershwins wrote for their first movie was "They Can't Take That Away from Me," and the next Astaire movie score included "A Foggy Day." At the time of his death Gershwin was working on a movie score that included the song "Love Is Here to Stay." Gershwin died in his prime at the age of thirty-eight from a brain tumor. He left us with a collection of hundreds of songs that have become part of our language and are heard today in concert halls, theaters, clubs, and on recordings throughout the world.

Duke Ellington (1899–1974)
Chelsea Bridge (Billy Strayhorn),
Lush Life (Billy Strayhorn),
Prelude to a Kiss, Satin Doll, Sophisticated Lady

Edward Kennedy ("Duke") Ellington grew up Washington, D.C., where as a child he occasionally practiced the piano but really preferred baseball. Then on a vacation he heard a piano player whose skill he envied, and Duke began practicing in earnest. He composed one of his first pieces, "Soda Fountain Rag," and enjoyed the attention he attracted when he played it. He started getting a few jobs playing the piano for parties and enjoyed this enough that he printed a "Music for All Occasions" advertisement. He was soon sending out four or five bands a night. Ellington learned music at this point mainly by ear but studied a little harmony with Doc Perry and Henry Grant.

Ellington and his band, The Washingtonians, wanted to find musical employment in Harlem, which they thought had the "world's most glamorous atmosphere." Fats Waller suggested that they come to New York to take over a job that he was quitting. This job never materialized for the band but they did manage to find employment at a club called Barron's. Their next job was at the Kentucky Club, where they played as a six-piece band for four years. Irving Mills, the music publisher, heard the band at the Kentucky Club and began to record them. Then in 1927 Ellington's band landed a job at the famous Cotton Club, the top place to go in Harlem. This job was very important for the band because they were heard nationally and internationally on a radio show broadcast from the Cotton Club. During this period the Ellington band also played in *Show Girl*, which George Gershwin had scored; accompanied Maurice Chevalier in a concert; and went to Hollywood to appear in a film featuring Amos 'n' Andy. These activities were arranged by Irving Mills, who was managing as well as recording the band at this point. Ellington composed songs that became big hits, such as "Mood Indigo," and even recorded a piece for Mills that was longer than three minutes, *Creole Rhapsody*, the seed for the extended works he was to compose later in his career.

Mills' next coup was getting the Ellington Orchestra to play at the London Palladium, then regarded as the top variety theater in the world. The orchestra was given a terrific reception and even had a jam session with the Prince of Wales sitting in on drums. On their return to the States, the band made a tour of the South and played at the Cotton Club and the Apollo Theater. During these years Ellington composed songs such as "In a Sentimental Mood," "Solitude," "Caravan," and "Don't Get Around Much Anymore." He composed the eloquent "Sophisticated Lady" in 1933 and his great "Prelude to a Kiss" in 1938. Ellington and Irving Mills parted ways in 1939, and Ellington signed on with the William Morris Agency.

Many of the Ellington band songs were composed by or in collaboration with Billy Strayhorn. Strayhorn composed the band's theme song "Take the 'A' Train," and two of the songs heard here, "Chelsea Bridge" and "Lush Life." In his autobiography, *Music Is My Mistress*, Ellington says Strayhorn "was my right arm, my left arm, all the eyes in the back of my head, my brainwaves in his head, and his in mine."

Soloists were also of vital importance to Ellington's composing, and many of his pieces were composed in collaboration with them. Tyree Glen, trombonist in the Ellington band, stated: "Duke listens to you carefully for a couple of months until he knows your sound and all your capabilities—and limitations, even though you may think he hasn't given you the opportunity yet to show what you can do. Then he writes a piece of music that is so precisely tailored to you that he teaches you things about yourself you never knew."

Ellington by his own admission also had quite a career as a

gourmand. His father was a caterer, his mother was an excellent cook, and the family placed emphasis on dining on the best food. In his autobiography, Duke devotes a whole chapter, entitled "Taste Buds," to a description of the different foods he enjoyed on his many tours with his band throughout the world. He loved crab meat and terrapin (see page 157), and especially liked a Parisian restaurant that served an omelet which from his description sounds exactly like the one presented here on page 46. He also discusses a restaurant he enjoyed in Holland that served ninety-nine hors d'oeuvres! He loved drinking, and in his autobiography calls himself a "retired juicehead" who "drank more booze than anybody ever."

In 1943 Ellington composed "Black, Brown, and Beige" for the first of a series of annual Carnegie Hall concerts. He was commissioned to write pieces for many symphony orchestras and was proclaimed by Stokowski, Stravinsky, and Milhaud to be one of the greatest modern composers. Ellington composed a wealth of material for the Newport and Monterey Jazz Festivals, and his first movie score, *Anatomy of a Murder*, was composed in 1959. He premiered his Sacred Concert in San Francisco's Grace Cathedral in 1965. The Sacred Concert was given performances in many cities throughout the world, and Duke Ellington felt this was one of the most important things he had ever done. Ellington became an ambassador of the United States on his State Department Tours, and he was awarded the highest civilian award of the United States, the Presidential Medal of Freedom. Duke Ellington was one of America's greatest and most prolific composers, and an excellent pianist, arranger, and conductor. The world will be forever indebted to him for, in William Blake's phrase, "catching joy as it flies."

CHINA MOON CAFE

Barbara Tropp opened her China Moon Cafe in March 1986. The restaurant is located in downtown San Francisco in what was originally the Paradise Coffee Shop early in the century. Barbara retained the original lunch counter, lighting, booths, wood paneling, and windows, and she extends this ambience by playing music from the 1930s in the restaurant. The techniques and most of the ingredients used in the open kitchen are Chinese (except for the desserts), but the dishes are not traditional Chinese. The cuisine is instead a very personal and inventive statement by Tropp.

Barbara Tropp is the author of *The Modern Art of Chinese Cooking* (Morrow). The appetizers presented here by *Menus and Music* are among the most popular dishes served at her restaurant.

∧ ∧ ∧ ∧ ∧

MENU

TEA AND SPICE SMOKED POUSSINS

MA-LA CUCUMBER FANS

STRANGE-FLAVOR EGGPLANT WITH
CROUTONS

FIRE-DRIED WALNUTS

ORCHID'S TANGY COOL NOODLES

TEA AND SPICE SMOKED POUSSINS

Poussins are baby chickens, and this is one of the many ways we serve them at China Moon Cafe. Being intensely flavorful, they are ideal paired with cold noodles and pickles. Count one-half *poussin* per person, and be sure to invite people who relish eating with their fingers! The brown Szechwan peppercorns and the Japanese sesame oil can be found in Asian markets.

6 to 10 fresh *poussins*, wing tips, tail, neck, and fat sacs removed

Roasted Szechwan Pepper-Salt*, 1 teaspoon per *poussin*

Finger lengths of green and white green onion, ¼ teaspoon per *poussin*

Thin coins of fresh ginger

Finely minced fresh ginger, ¼ teaspoon per *poussin*

Finely minced fresh orange zest**, ¼ teaspoon per *poussin*

SMOKING MIXTURE

¼ cup dry, fragrant black tea leaves

¼ cup dry rice

¼ cup packed light brown sugar

1 tablespoon crumbed cassia bark or cinnamon stick

2 whole star anise, broken into 16 points

1 tablespoon brown Szechwan peppercorns

Japanese sesame oil to gloss

Rinse each bird inside and out, then pat dry. Sprinkle the cavity and outside of each bird generously with the pepper-salt. Stuff each cavity with several pieces of green onion and a coin of ginger, then sprinkle the breasts and legs lightly with the minced ginger and orange zest. Seal airtight and refrigerate overnight to marinate.

Drain the birds of accumulated juices, then steam them for 15 minutes. Remove to a plate until cool enough to handle.

Line a wok and its lid each with a generous piece of heavy-duty aluminum foil. Combine the smoking ingredients and spread in the bottom of the wok. Place the *poussins* breast-side up on an oiled cookie rack that will sit in the wok an inch above the smoking ingredients, then fit the rack in the wok.

Turn the heat to its highest under the wok. Once the sugar begins to burn and several thick plumes of smoke begin to appear, 3 to 10 minutes depending upon your stove***, fit the lid on the wok, and roll the edges of foil together to trap the smoke inside the wok.

Smoke the *poussins* for 8 minutes, then turn off the heat and let them rest in the covered wok for 5 minutes. Remove the lid, carefully transfer the birds to a platter, then brush lightly with sesame oil to gloss.

To serve, cut off the wings and drumsticks, cut each bird in half through the breast, discard the backbone, then cut each breast crosswise into 4 rectangular pieces for easy eating with chopsticks or fingers.

YIELD: 12 TO 20 SERVINGS

* Roasted Szechwan Pepper-Salt is our all-purpose seasoning at China Moon Cafe. To make, toast ½ cup coarse kosher salt and ¼ cup brown Szechwan peppercorns in a dry skillet over moderate heat, stirring until the salt turns off-white, about 5 minutes. Lower the heat if the peppercorns begin to scorch; expect them, however, to smoke. Grind the hot mixture to a powder, then sieve to remove the peppercorn husks.

** For good-flavored fresh orange zest, the oranges must first be washed in hot, soapy water with an abrasive scrubber, then rinsed and dried. This is to remove wax and pesticides commonly used by the commercial orange industry.

*** If using a gas stove, invert the burner grid and nest the wok directly on top in order to bring it closest to the flame. On an electric stove, sit the wok directly on the coil.

Note: Smoked *poussins* may be served hot from the smoker or cool. For the best flavor, do not refrigerate before serving and do not re-heat.

MA-LA CUCUMBER FANS

These crispy cucumber fans are fun to make and great fun to eat. They are a wonderful crunchy nibble on their own—at the restaurant, they are our best-selling "food to make the wine go down"— and are also perfect when paired with cold noodles or smoked poultry. For best results, use the very thin, sweet, and seedless Japanese cucumbers available in Asian markets and make the fans a day or more in advance. The sesame oil, peppercorns, and rice vinegar are also found in Asian markets.

1 pound firm Japanese, kirby, or Armenian cucumbers

2 teaspoons coarse kosher salt

AROMATICS

1 tablespoon finely minced garlic

2 tablespoons very finely julienned (thread thin) fresh ginger

½ teaspoon brown Szechwan peppercorns

½ teaspoon dried red chili flakes

LIQUIDS

2 tablespoons unseasoned Japanese rice vinegar

3 tablespoons sugar

1 teaspoon soy sauce

1 tablespoon corn or peanut oil

Several drops Japanese sesame oil

Remove the tips from the cucumbers and cut the cucumbers into 2-inch lengths. Grasping one segment at a time between chopsticks placed scissor-like on your workboard, cut the cucumbers with a small knife crosswise at $\frac{1}{16}$-inch intervals down to the chopsticks. (Chopsticks prevent the knife from cutting through, thus making the fan.) Put the cucumber fans in a large bowl, sprinkle with the salt, then toss to mix. Let stand 60 minutes at room temperature. Rinse the fans with cold water, then drain well.

Mix together the aromatics and the liquids in separate bowls. Heat a wok or large heavy skillet over high heat until hot enough to evaporate a bead of water. Add the oils, swirl to glaze, then reduce the heat to medium high. Add the aromatics and stir gently until fully fragrant, adjusting the heat so they foam without scorching and adding more oil if needed to prevent sticking.

Add the cucumbers, toss to combine, then stir the liquids and add to the pan. Toss until the liquids begin to steam in a near-simmer, then turn off the heat.

Remove the cucumbers cut-side down to a shallow dish, then scrape the liquids on the top. Let stand until cool, then cover and refrigerate overnight for the best flavor. Serve at room temperature, fan-side up, with a bit of juice and the aromatics on top.

YIELD: 8 TO 12 HORS D'OEUVRES

Note: The fans will keep well 4 to 5 days refrigerated. The juice cannot be used again.

STRANGE-FLAVOR EGGPLANT
WITH CROUTONS

This is one of the favorite dishes at China Moon Cafe. It is tangy, lightly sweet and spicy all at once, and is equally nice served with croutons or spooned into hearts of assorted lettuces.

One 1- to 1¼-pound Western eggplant

AROMATICS

1 tablespoon finely minced garlic

1 tablespoon finely minced fresh ginger

3 tablespoons thin-cut green and white green onion rings

¼ to ½ teaspoon dried red chili flakes

LIQUIDS

3 tablespoons soy sauce

3 tablespoons packed light brown sugar

1 teaspoon unseasoned Japanese rice vinegar*

1 tablespoon hot water

2½ tablespoons corn or peanut oil

1 teaspoon Japanese sesame oil*

* Available in Asian markets

CROUTONS

Sweet baguettes cut thinly on the diagonal

Corn or peanut oil infused with garlic and ginger

Green and white green onion rings

Preheat the oven to 475°. Remove the leaves from the eggplant. Prick the flesh with a fork and bake until soft when pressed, about 20 minutes. Turn the eggplant over midway through baking. Let it cool, peel, then process the pulp in a blender or food processor to a near-purée, retaining a bit of texture.

Combine the aromatics on a plate. Combine the liquids in a small bowl, stirring to dissolve the sugar.

Heat a wok or heavy skillet over high heat until hot enough to evaporate a bead of water. Add the corn or peanut oil, swirl the pan to glaze it, and then reduce heat to medium-high. Add the aromatics and stir until fully fragrant, about 20 seconds, adjusting the heat so they foam without browning.

Stir the liquids, add to the pan, and stir gently to bring to a simmer. Add the eggplant and stir to combine and heat through. Turn off the heat and adjust as required with an extra bit of sugar, soy, chili, or vinegar to get a zesty taste with a round spiciness. (Eggplants differ enormously, so expect to need to adjust.) Sprinkle with the sesame oil, stir to combine, then scrape the eggplant into a shallow bowl to cool. To make the croutons, brush the baguette slices with the flavored oil and toast until golden. Serve the eggplant tepid or slightly chilled, garnished with green onion rings and accompanied with croutons.

YIELD: ABOUT 2 CUPS

FIRE-DRIED WALNUTS

A typical Hunanese home-style nibble, this little dish is also lovely when done with pecans. At China Moon Cafe, it is especially loved with a flute of dry champagne.

½ pound (2 cups) very plump fresh walnut halves

2 teaspoons corn or peanut oil

½ teaspoon coarse kosher salt

2 tablespoons sugar

Put the nuts in a large heatproof bowl, cover with boiling water, then let stand for 30 minutes. (Soaking the nuts rids them of bitter oils in addition to changing the texture.) Drain, spray with cool water to rinse, then drain again.

Preheat the oven to 275°. Towel-dry the nuts, then spread them on a jelly-roll pan and bake until crisp with just a touch of moistness at the core, about 20 minutes. Stir occasionally while drying.

Heat a wok or large heavy skillet over high heat until hot enough to evaporate a bead of water. Add the oil, swirl to glaze the pan, then reduce the heat to medium. Add the nuts and toss to coat until they are warm to the touch, reducing the heat further if needed to prevent scorching.

Sprinkle the nuts with the salt, toss until it is dissolved, then sprinkle at intervals with sugar, tossing to allow the first teaspoons of sugar to dissolve before adding the next, about 3 to 4 minutes total.

Serve hot from the pan or cooled, in a bowl of contrasting color.

YIELD: 2 CUPS

Note: These nuts may be done well ahead. Let them cool, then store in an airtight bottle. Do not re-warm to serve.

ORCHID'S TANGY COOL NOODLES

My Chinese name is Precious Orchid, and this is the first dish I ever made. It has a (to me) nearly inexplicable popularity. At China Moon Cafe, it is often featured as part of our Peking Antipasto, served along with Tea and Spice Smoked Poussins and Ma-La Cucumber Fans.

1 pound 1/16-inch-thin fresh or frozen Chinese or Italian egg noodles

LIQUIDS

3½ tablespoons Japanese sesame oil

3½ tablespoons black soy sauce

1½ tablespoons Chinese black vinegar or balsamic vinegar

2 tablespoons sugar

2 teaspoons coarse kosher salt

½ to 1 tablespoon hot chili oil

4 heaping tablespoons thick-cut green and white green onion rings
More green onion rings to garnish

Fluff the noodles to separate the strands. Cook in an ample amount of lightly salted boiling water until *al dente*, only a minute or so for fresh noodles. Drain promptly and flush with cold running water until thoroughly chilled. Drain well, then put the noodles in a large bowl.

Stir the liquids to combine, then toss well with the noodles, using your hands to coat and separate the strands. Add the green onion rings and toss again to mix.

continued

Taste and adjust with a dash more chili oil or sugar to obtain a round spiciness. Serve in a large bowl of contrasting color, garnished with a fresh sprinkling of green onion rings.

YIELD: 8 TO 12 FIRST-COURSE SERVINGS

Note: These noodles may be refrigerated for several days prior to serving, and are actually best the second day once the flavors have had time to marry. If making them in advance, expect them to grow spicier. Let them come to room temperature and re-toss before serving. The sesame oil, black soy sauce and vinegar, and the chili oil are all available in Asian markets.

BAY WOLF

RESTAURANT & CAFE

The Bay Wolf restaurant has been serving a blend of traditional French- and Italian-based dishes with a California touch for the past eleven years in Oakland. The menu changes daily and consists of a selection of appetizers and five innovative entrees. The restaurant also features Spanish food and serves *tapas* such as the following ones prepared for *Menus and Music*. These recipes were created by chef Carol Brendlinger, who composes the restaurant's imaginative theme dinners such as an Elizabethan dinner to benefit the Early Music Society of San Francisco and a jazz dinner to benefit a Jazz in the Classroom project. Carol notes that "music and food have been associated for millenia. The Bay Wolf is proud to nourish that on-going relationship."

∧ ∧ ∧ ∧ ∧

MENU

GARLIC-TOASTED ALMONDS AND
HAZELNUTS

VARIOUS MARINATED OLIVES

EMPANADILLAS DE PATO

BANDAS

ENDIBIAS RELLENAS

PESCADOS FRITOS

BROCHETAS OF LAMB AND TONGUE

ARTICHOKE ALLIOLI AND SALSA
ROMESCO

BABY ARTICHOKES, GREEN BEANS,
ASPARAGUS, TOMATOES

TORTILLA DE CANGREJO

PATATAS RELLENAS CON BACALAO

TARTALETAS DE GAMBA

*SELECTION OF FINO AND AMONTILLADO
SHERRIES*

BAY WOLF

EMPANADILLAS DE PATO

Empanadillas de pato are turnovers of duck, spinach, and pine nuts served with a spiced pear sauce.

PEAR SAUCE

2 pounds pears, peeled, cored, and quartered

1 cup dry sherry

1 cup sherry wine vinegar

1 cinnamon stick

6 garlic cloves, sliced

3 shallots, sliced

1 tablespoon minced fresh ginger

1 teaspoon dried red chili flakes

FILLING

1 red onion, cut into small dice

3 garlic cloves, minced

1 red bell pepper, cut into small dice

¼ cup extra-virgin Spanish olive oil

½ cup pine nuts

¼ cup currants

1 cup dry sherry

2 cups cooked duck meat, cut into small dice

2 bunches spinach, cooked, squeezed dry, and chopped

2 pounds fresh or thawed frozen puff pastry

1 egg beaten with 2 tablespoons water

Combine all the sauce ingredients in an enamel-coated or stainless steel saucepan. Simmer until the pears are tender, 30 to 45 minutes. Remove the cinnamon stick. Purée in a food mill, blender, or food processor.

To make the filling, in a sauté pan or skillet, sauté the onion, garlic, and red pepper in the olive oil until translucent. Add the pine nuts and sauté 1 minute. Add the currants and sherry. Evaporate the liquid. Let cool. Mix with the duck meat and spinach. Correct the seasoning.

Preheat the oven to 450°. Roll out the puff pastry ⅛ inch thick. Cut into 3-inch squares. Put 1 tablespoon filling on each square and fold over on the diagonal. Seal with a few drops of water. Brush with the beaten egg and chill. Bake for 10 minutes. Turn the oven down to 350°. Bake 10 minutes more. Serve as soon as possible, with the pear sauce on the side.

YIELD: 15 TO 25 TAPAS

BANDAS

Bandas are ribbon tarts of roasted peppers, anchovies, and olives.

6 red and yellow bell peppers

1 pound fresh or thawed frozen puff pastry

4 garlic cloves, minced

2 tablespoons extra-virgin Spanish olive oil

¼ pound softened goat cheese (optional)

2 ounces Spanish anchovies*, packed in salt

2 cups green and black olives, pitted and chopped

Char the peppers under a broiler or over an open flame until blackened all over. Place in a closed paper bag until cool, then rub off the skin. Halve, seed, and cut the peppers into long strips.

Roll the puff pastry into a rectangle ⅛ inch thick, 8 inches wide and about 16 inches long. Cut into two 4-inch strips. Cut off a ½-inch band on each side. Brush cold water on the edges of the strips and lay the bands of dough along the edges to make the rims of the tarts. Press to seal the rims. Prick the centers with a fork. Chill.

In a sauté pan or skillet, simmer the garlic in the olive oil for 15 minutes. Preheat the oven to 450°. Toss the peppers with the garlic and set aside. Spread a layer of goat cheese over the pastry, if you like. Arrange the peppers on the tart shells in long ribbons, alternating colors. Garnish with anchovies and olives. Bake for 15 minutes. Turn the oven down to 375° and bake 15 minutes more. Slice each tart into fifteen 1-inch pieces. Serve hot or cool.

YIELD: 30 TAPAS

* The anchovies can be soaked in cold water to reduce their saltiness, if desired.

ENDIBIAS RELLENAS

Endibias rellenas are Belgian endives stuffed with a red pepper-almond filling.

3 large medium-hot red peppers, or 3 red bell peppers and
   1 *jalapeño*
1 red onion, sliced
6 garlic cloves, minced
½ cup extra-virgin Spanish olive oil
½ cup vinegar
1 cup lightly toasted almonds*
Salt
4 to 6 endives
Chopped fresh chives

Seed, devein, and slice the peppers. In a sauté pan or skillet, sauté the peppers, onion, and garlic in the olive oil until translucent. Add the vinegar and boil rapidly until the liquid evaporates. Grind the almonds in a blender or food processor. Add the peppers and purée to a thick paste. Salt to taste. Separate the endives into leaves. Spread the paste on the leaves. Garnish with chives.

YIELD: ABOUT 40 TAPAS

* To toast the almonds, stir them in a dry skillet over medium heat until just golden.

PESCADOS FRITOS

Pescados fritos are small deep-fried fish in a cornmeal-beer batter.

BATTER

1 cup all-purpose flour

1 cup stone-ground cornmeal

3 cups beer

1 tablespoon salt

1 teaspoon Tabasco sauce

Oil for deep-frying*

2 to 3 pounds of any small fish (fresh anchovies, whitebait, squid, shrimp, or finger-sized slices of seabass, sole, etc.)

Whisk all the ingredients for the batter together. Chill for 30 minutes. The batter should be just thick enough to coat the fish.

Heat the oil in a deep heavy pot to 340°. Dip the fish into the batter and fry in small batches until crisp. Drain on paper towels. Serve hot.

YIELD: ABOUT 40 TAPAS

* Preferably a mix of ½ olive oil and ½ peanut oil, although you must be careful not to let the oil overheat.

BROCHETAS OF LAMB AND TONGUE

MARINADE

1 cup olive oil

½ cup dry red wine

2 tablespoons paprika

6 garlic cloves, minced

2 pounds trimmed lamb from loin or leg

2 pounds lamb or veal tongue, cooked and peeled

2 red bell peppers, seeded and deveined

2 bunches green onions, trimmed

Mix together the marinade ingredients. Cut the meats into 1-inch cubes. Place in a nonmetal container, pour the marinade over, and marinate for 1 hour.

Light the charcoal for an open grill or preheat the broiler. Cut the peppers into 1-inch squares. Cut the green onions into 1-inch lengths. Put one piece of lamb and one piece of tongue on a skewer, alternating with the pepper and onion. Grill. Serve immediately.

YIELD: 30 TO 40 TAPAS

ARTICHOKE ALLIOLI

Artichoke *allioli*, a Catalan version of *aïoli*, can be used as a dipping sauce for fried fish, vegetables, and the *brochetas* on the preceding page.

3 large artichokes

1 lemon half

¼ cup distilled white vinegar

12 garlic cloves

1½ teaspoons salt

3 egg yolks

2 cups extra-virgin Spanish olive oil

¼ cup fresh lemon juice

Cut off the base of the artichokes and break off all the leaves up to the top third; cut off the top with a sharp knife. Trim off all the green and cut out the choke. Rub all over with the lemon. Add the vinegar to a large pot of boiling salted water and cook the artichoke hearts until tender, about 30 minutes.

Purée the artichoke hearts in a food mill, blender, or food processor and set aside. In a large mixing bowl, mash the garlic and salt together. Whisk in the egg yolks, then whisk in the olive oil drop by drop until the sauce is emulsified. Stir in the lemon juice and artichoke purée. Correct the seasoning.

YIELD: ABOUT 3 CUPS

SALSA ROMESCO

This sauce is used as a dipping sauce for fried fish, vegetables, and *brochetas*.

6 dried New Mexico or other dried large mild red chilies

1½ cups water

1 cup red wine vinegar

½ cup slivered blanched almonds, toasted*

8 garlic cloves minced with 1½ teaspoons salt

1 cup bread crumbs

1½ cups extra-virgin Spanish olive oil

3 tomatoes, peeled and seeded

Simmer the chilies in the water and vinegar until softened. Drain the chilies, reserving the cooking liquid. Remove the seeds and stems. Purée the chilies in a blender or food processor. Add the almonds and garlic. Purée to a paste. In a sauté pan or skillet, fry the bread crumbs in ½ cup of the olive oil. Add to the blender along with the tomatoes and reserved cooking liquid. Purée. Add the rest of the olive oil slowly through the top of the blender while it is running. The sauce will emulsify and should be fairly thick. If you like a hotter sauce, use hotter chilies or add dried red chili flakes.

YIELD: ABOUT 3 CUPS

* To toast the almonds, stir them in a dry skillet over medium heat until golden.

TORTILLA DE CANGREJO

Tortilla de cangrejo is a crab and chorizo omelet.

2 onions, cut into small dice

4 garlic cloves, minced

½ pound Spanish chorizo or Cajun *andouille*, cut into small dice

½ cup extra-virgin Spanish olive oil

2 tomatoes, peeled, seeded, and chopped

9 eggs

½ pound fresh cooked crab meat

In a sauté pan or skillet, sauté the onions, garlic, and chorizo in 2 tablespoons of the olive oil until translucent. Add the tomatoes and cook rapidly to evaporate excess moisture. Cool. In a large mixing bowl, beat the eggs and mix in the crab and sausage-tomato mixture. Heat an 8-inch sauté pan or skillet very hot. Add 2 tablespoons of the olive oil and pour in one-third of the egg mixture. Lower the heat and cook until the bottom is brown. Turn the omelet over and cook until brown on the other side. Remove to a platter. Repeat with the other 2 batches. Cut the omelets into cubes and serve at room temperature.

YIELD: ABOUT 40 TAPAS

PATATAS RELLENAS CON BACALAO

Patatas rellenas con bacalao are baked potatoes stuffed with a salt cod salad.

SALAD

1 pound salt cod, soaked overnight and drained

3 garlic cloves, minced

¼ cup fresh lemon juice

½ cup extra-virgin Spanish olive oil

2 red bell peppers, seeded, deveined, and minced

1 bunch green onions, minced

20 small thin-skinned white or red potatoes, halved

20 cherry tomatoes, halved

Preheat the oven to 400°. Place the salt cod in a large pot, add water to cover, and bring to a boil. Remove from the heat, drain, and shred. Mix the fish with the rest of the salad ingredients and set aside.

Bake the potatoes until tender and crisp, about 25 minutes. Hollow out the centers and fill with the salad. Top with a cherry tomato half. Serve hot or at room temperature.

YIELD: 40 TAPAS

TARTALETAS DE GAMBA

Tartaletas de gamba are shrimp, ham, and dandelion tartlets.

PATE A CHOUX

1½ cups water

½ cup (1 stick) butter

Salt and pepper to taste

1½ cups unbleached all-purpose flour

6 eggs

1 cup freshly grated Parmesan cheese

FILLING

1 bunch dandelion greens, sliced thin

¼ pound Westphalian ham or prosciutto, minced

6 garlic cloves, minced

1 large onion, cut into small dice

½ cup extra-virgin Spanish olive oil

2 pounds shrimp, peeled and deveined

2 egg whites

2 eggs, beaten

To make the tartlets, place the water in a heavy medium saucepan and bring it to a boil; add the butter and cook until melted. Add seasoning. Off heat, pour in all the flour and stir quickly to blend. Over medium-high heat, cook and stir the mixture until it leaves the side of the pan. Remove from the heat again. Break one egg into the pan and stir it rapidly into the mixture. Repeat one by one with the remaining eggs, then rapidly stir in the Parmesan cheese.

To make the filling, in a sauté pan or skillet, sauté the greens, ham, garlic, and onion in the olive oil until translucent. Cool. Cut the shrimp into ½-inch pieces. Coat with the egg whites. Toss with the greens mixture and set aside.

Preheat the oven to 425°. Place the *pâte* in a pastry bag with a plain tip and pipe in 2-inch rounds on buttered baking sheets. Press a tablespoon of filling in the center of each tart. Brush the tops with the beaten eggs. Bake for 15 minutes. Serve immediately.

YIELD: ABOUT 30 TAPAS

THE
CALIFORNIA
CULINARY
ACADEMY

The California Culinary Academy is an internationally acclaimed school for chefs as well as a restaurant. It was founded in 1977 by Danielle Carlisle Walker and is now one of the Big Three culinary schools in the nation. The Academy's objective is to educate students in the art of professional cookery, with emphasis on the preparation of classical cuisine and with instruction provided by European-trained chefs. The public is invited to the Academy's restaurant so that the students may benefit from immediate application of their newly acquired skills and participate in the day-to-day operation of a restaurant. These hors d'oeuvres recipes for *Menus and Music* were created at the Academy by Executive Chef Roberto Gerometta.

∧ ∧ ∧ ∧ ∧

MENU

BLINIS AU CAVIAR

ARTICHOKES WITH CHERVIL

ARTICHOKES A LA GRECQUE

COLD ASPARAGUS WITH SWEET-PEPPER
VINAIGRETTE

FRIED CAMEMBERT

BLINIS AU CAVIAR

1½ cups buckwheat flour (or 1 cup buckwheat flour and ½ cup fine
    groats, pulverized)

1 teaspoon sugar

½ teaspoon salt

1 egg

1 egg yolk

2 tablespoons unsalted butter, melted and cooled

½ package yeast dissolved in ¼ cup lukewarm water

¼ cup lukewarm milk, plus more if necessary

Salted butter (for omelet pan)

Red and/or black caviar

1 cup sour cream

½ cup warm clarified unsalted butter (see page 75)

Sift together the flour, sugar, and salt. Mix together the egg and egg
yolk, melted butter, yeast dissolved in water, and lukewarm milk.
Mix together with a whisk until quite smooth. Add enough more
lukewarm milk to bring the batter to the consistency of heavy
cream. Cover with a cloth; let rise 30 minutes in a warm place.

Heat an omelet pan very hot. Wipe the pan with salted butter,
using a wad of waxed paper. Spoon a large tablespoon of the batter
into the pan and spread it thin, to about 4 inches in diameter. Brown
one side, then the other. Make all the *blini* this way.

To serve, cover a platter with a warm napkin and put the *blini* on
it. Accompany it with little bowls of red and/or black caviar and
sour cream, and a little copper pan of warm clarified butter.

YIELD: HORS D'OEUVRES FOR 6 PEOPLE

ARTICHOKES WITH CHERVIL

6 medium artichokes

1 lemon, cut in half

½ cup white wine vinegar

2 tablespoons butter

1 shallot, minced

3 tablespoons dry white wine

¾ cup *crème fraîche* (see page 123)

1 tablespoon Dijon mustard

Salt and fresh-ground white pepper

2 tablespoons minced fresh chervil

Cut off the base of the artichokes and break off all the leaves up to the top third; cut off the top with a sharp knife. Trim off all the green with a sharp knife and cut out the choke. Rub all over with the cut lemon. Add the vinegar to a large pot of boiling water; add the artichokes and cook until tender, about 30 minutes. Drain and set aside.

Melt the butter in a sauté pan or skillet and sauté the shallot until translucent. Add the artichokes, pour in the white wine, and cook a few minutes. Remove the artichokes with a slotted spoon. Add the *crème fraîche* and cook until slightly reduced. Add the mustard and salt and pepper to taste; stir in the chervil. Thinly slice the artichokes and arrange on plates. Pour the sauce over the artichokes.

YIELD: 6 FIRST-COURSE SERVINGS

ARTICHOKES A LA GRECQUE

15 to 20 baby artichokes, or 5 large artichokes

MARINADE

4½ cups water

⅝ cup vegetable oil

Juice of 3 lemons

1 teaspoon salt

¼ cup chopped fennel

¼ cup chopped celery

10 coriander seeds

10 peppercorns

Fresh thyme sprig

2 bay leaves

Trim the bases of the baby artichokes. Pull off the outer leaves and cut the top of each off bluntly with a large knife. If using large artichokes, trim into hearts (see page 55) and cut each into 3 or 4 sections. Blanch the artichokes in boiling salted water to cover for 5 to 7 minutes, or until easily pierced with a knife. If cooking artichoke hearts, rub with cut lemon and cook in acidulated water (see page 55) until tender. Drain the artichokes and plunge them into cold water.

In a stockpot, mix together all the marinade ingredients. Bring the marinade to a boil for a few minutes, then add the artichokes and cook gently for 15 minutes. Allow the artichokes to cool in the marinade, and serve a little of the marinade with the artichokes.

YIELD: 15 TO 20 ARTICHOKES

COLD ASPARAGUS WITH SWEET-PEPPER VINAIGRETTE

48 asparagus spears

1 tablespoon Dijon mustard

1 egg yolk

¼ cup sherry vinegar

1 cup olive oil

1 cup peanut oil

1 tablespoon chopped garlic

½ cup each yellow, red, and green bell pepper strips

Salt and pepper to taste

1 tablespoon capers, drained

Trim the asparagus and cook them in boiling salted water to cover until tender, about 5 to 8 minutes. Drain and plunge into cold water.

Whisk together the mustard, egg yolk, and vinegar. Slowly whisk in the olive oil, then the peanut oil. Add the garlic, peppers, salt and pepper, and capers. Pour the vinaigrette over the asparagus just before serving.

YIELD: HORS D'OEUVRES FOR 16 PEOPLE

FRIED CAMEMBERT

1½ baskets fresh raspberries

BATTER

1 egg
¾ cup all-purpose flour
Milk
Salt to taste

Oil for deep-frying
One 8-ounce round Camembert cheese
Radicchio leaves
Chopped fresh chives

Purée 1 basket raspberries in a blender or food processor and set aside. Reserve the remaining raspberries for garnish. To make the batter, beat the egg in a mixing bowl and stir in the flour. Add milk to make a batter the consistency of heavy cream. Add salt. Chill for 30 minutes.

Heat the oil to 350°. Dip the cheese in the batter and deep-fry until lightly browned. Pool the raspberry purée on a large plate and top with a bed of *radicchio*. Top the *radicchio* with the cheese and garnish with chives and reserved raspberries.

YIELD: HORS D'OEUVRES FOR 8 PEOPLE

Carnelian Room

The Carnelian Room sits fifty-two floors atop the Bank of America Center in San Francisco's financial district. Restaurant patrons enjoy a magnificent view of the entire Bay Area while dining on seasonal American cuisine. By changing the menu with each equinox, the chef can prepare foods at the peak of freshness and succulence. The Carnelian Room wine cellar, which houses the finest domestic and imported wines and specializes in California wineries, has been honored with the "Grand Award" from *The Wine Spectator* as one of the best in the country. The restaurant also offers eight private dining suites for groups of two to one thousand.

∧ ∧ ∧ ∧ ∧

MENU

OYSTER FRITTERS WITH CUCUMBER
CUPS AND RED-PEPPER MAYONNAISE

CRAB CAKES WITH JALAPENO SAUCE

GOAT CHEESE WITH LEEKS AND A
BOUQUET OF HERBS

SNOW PEAS STUFFED WITH CAVIAR AND
CREME FRAICHE

SAUTE OF WILD MUSHROOMS WITH
SWEET PEPPER, GARLIC, AND FILO PASTRY

CHICKEN LIVER MOUSSE WITH ROAST
PISTACHIOS

OYSTER FRITTERS WITH CUCUMBER CUPS AND RED-PEPPER MAYONNAISE

1½ pints shucked fresh oysters

1 quart vegetable oil

1½ cups sifted all-purpose flour

½ teaspoon salt

¼ teaspoon baking powder

2 eggs, beaten

⅓ cup milk

⅓ cup reserved oyster liquor

4 English cucumbers

Red-Pepper Mayonnaise, following

2 chives, chopped

Drain the oysters, reserving the oyster liquor. Chop the oysters and set them aside. Heat the vegetable oil in a deep-fryer or a large heavy saucepan to 375°.

Stir the flour, salt, and baking powder together in a mixing bowl. Stir in the eggs, milk, and oyster liquor. Fold in the chopped oysters. Drop the batter by heaping teaspoons, a few at a time, into the oil. Fry until browned, turning once, about 5 minutes in all. Remove the fritters with a slotted spoon and drain on paper towels. This must be done in several batches so that the pan is not too full. Allow the oil to regain the correct temperature between batches.

To make the cucumber cups, peel the cucumbers and cut them in 1-inch slices. Remove the insides halfway down with a melon ball cutter. Salt the cups and turn them upside down to drain for a few minutes.

To assemble, put the cucumber cups on a plate, pour some Red-Pepper Mayonnaise in each cup, and arrange the little fritters on top. Garnish with a piece of chive.

YIELD: ABOUT 24 HORS D'OEUVRES

RED-PEPPER MAYONNAISE

1 teaspoon olive oil

1 medium onion, sliced

2 red bell peppers, chopped

1 teaspoon paprika

Cayenne to taste

½ cup dry white wine

1 cup mayonnaise

½ cup heavy cream, whipped

Heat the olive oil in a large sauté pan or skillet. Sauté the onion until translucent. Add the red peppers, paprika, cayenne, white wine, and salt. Cook for about 15 minutes. Purée in a blender or food processor. Add the mayonnaise. Remove the mixture from the blender or food processor, and let it cool for a few minutes. Fold in the whipped cream very delicately.

YIELD: ABOUT 2½ CUPS

CRAB CAKES WITH JALAPENO SAUCE

4 tablespoons unsalted butter

¼ cup chopped shallots

¼ cup Pernod

½ cup *crème fraîche* (see page 123) or heavy cream

½ tablespoon butter, blended into a paste with ½ tablespoon flour

¾ teaspoon salt

¼ teaspoon ground white pepper

1 pound fresh cooked crab meat, picked over and shredded

4 eggs, beaten

4 cups white egg-bread crumbs (preferably fresh)

1½ cups clarified butter (see page 75)

24 lemon wedges

24 dill sprigs

Jalapeño Sauce, following

Melt the butter in a sauté pan or skillet over moderate heat. Add the shallots and cook, stirring occasionally, until soft, 3 to 4 minutes. Add the Pernod, and cook for a few minutes. Add the *crème fraîche*, butter-flour paste, salt, and pepper, and stir to mix. Add the crab and stir gently until incorporated, then cook for 5 minutes. Do not burn. Remove to a large bowl and let cool to room temperature. Mix in the eggs.

Divide the crab mixture into 24 portions and form into 1-inch-thick patties. Coat evenly with the bread crumbs, pressing so they will adhere. Place the cakes on a rack and refrigerate until very firm, about 1 hour.

Pour the clarified butter into a heavy sauté pan or skillet to a depth of ½ inch. Heat to 365°, or until the fat begins to shimmer.

Fry a few of the crab cakes at a time, turning once, until well browned, about 4 minutes on each side. Remove with a slotted spoon and drain on paper towels. Repeat with the remaining crab cakes. The crab cakes can be held at room temperature for a few hours. Reheat in a preheated 325° oven for 12 to 15 minutes before serving.

Garnish with the lemon wedges and dill sprigs and serve hot with Jalapeño Sauce on the side.

YIELD: 24 CRAB CAKES

JALAPENO SAUCE

2 tablespoons olive oil

1 large onion, chopped

2 garlic cloves

2 *jalapeño* peppers, seeded, deveined, and chopped

1 cup dry white wine

1 cup heavy cream

3 green bell peppers, seeded, deveined, and chopped

Salt to taste

2½ teaspoons grated lemon zest

Heat the olive oil in a heavy sauté pan or skillet. Add the onion, garlic, *jalapeño*, white wine, and heavy cream and cook for 5 minutes. Add the green peppers and cook for 3 minutes. Purée in a blender or food processor. Season to taste and serve topped with the grated lemon zest alongside the crab cakes.

YIELD: ABOUT 2½ CUPS

GOAT CHEESE WITH LEEKS AND A BOUQUET OF HERBS

⅓ cup minced leeks

5 tablespoons unsalted butter, softened

3 ounces goat cheese

¼ cup cream cheese, softened

4 eggs

3 tablespoons sour cream

⅛ teaspoon salt

¼ teaspoon ground white pepper

8 fresh tarragon branches

8 fresh thyme branches

8 chives

Preheat the oven to 350°. Melt 2 tablespoons of the butter in a small pan and saute the leeks until tender.

In a blender, food processor, or mixing bowl, cream the goat cheese with the remaining 3 tablespoons of butter until very smooth. Add the cream cheese and blend in the eggs, one at a time, blending after each addition until the mixture is smooth. If the mixture is lumpy, strain before continuing. Add the sour cream, leeks, salt, and pepper. Mix well.

Pour the mixture into a buttered 8-inch pie pan and set the pie pan into a larger pan. Add enough hot water to come halfway up the sides of the pie pan. Bake until the mixture is firm, golden, and puffy, 20 to 25 minutes.

Cool to room temperature (the cake will collapse) and cut it into 16 wedges. Take a tarragon and thyme branch and make a bouquet, tying it together with a chive. Put an herb bouquet on top of each wedge.

YIELD: 16 HORS D'OEUVRES

SNOW PEAS STUFFED WITH CAVIAR AND CREME FRAICHE

20 young snow peas

3 tablespoons cream cheese, softened

6 tablespoons *crème fraîche* (see page 123)

1½ teaspoons fresh lemon juice

4 ounces large California golden caviar

½ bunch fresh dill

Blanch the peas in boiling salted water until tender, about 1 minute. Plunge them into cold water and drain. Slit the peas open on one side and set aside.

Combine the softened cream cheese, *crème fraîche*, and lemon juice. Carefully fold in 2 tablespoons of the caviar until just combined, being careful not to break the caviar eggs.

Spoon the filling into the pea pods and top each with some of the remaining caviar. Decorate with dill sprigs. Refrigerate for 1 hour before serving.

YIELD: 20 HORS D'OEUVRES

SAUTE OF WILD MUSHROOMS WITH SWEET PEPPER, GARLIC, AND FILO PASTRY

12 leaves fresh or frozen *filo*

2 tablespoons melted unsalted butter

2 ounces each *shiitake*, *enoki*, oyster, and common store mushrooms

2 teaspoons olive oil

1 garlic clove, minced

Salt and pepper to taste

2 teaspoons cognac

¼ bell pepper, cut in julienne

2 tablespoons shredded fresh basil

Defrost frozen *filo* the night before making the *filo* cups. To make the *filo* cups, preheat the oven to 375°. Turn muffin tins upside down (enough to make 18 cups) and butter the outsides. Take 2 leaves of *filo* and cut them into circles twice as large as the bottom of the muffin cups. Form them over the muffin cups. Lightly brush the top *filo* round with melted butter. Repeat 2 times for a total of 6 layers. Bake the *filo* until golden brown.

Wash and dry all the mushrooms and cut all but the *enokis* into quarters. Put the olive oil in a large sauté pan or skillet and heat until smoking. Sauté the *shiitake*, oyster, and store mushrooms, garlic, salt, and pepper for a few minutes. Deglaze with the cognac and add the bell pepper and basil. Divide the mushroom mixture among the *filo* cups. Garnish with the *enokis* and serve.

Yield: 18 cups

CHICKEN LIVER MOUSSE WITH
ROAST PISTACHIOS

1 cup pistachios, chopped

1 large onion, minced

4 shallots, chopped

5 tablespoons vegetable oil

1 pound chicken livers, trimmed, rinsed, and patted dry

4 bay leaves

¼ cup Armagnac

1 cup dry white wine

½ teaspoon red food coloring

Salt and white pepper to taste

3 cups heavy cream

2 leaves (2 by 6 inches) gelatin sheets, soaked in cool water,
   rinsed, and squeezed of excess water, or 1 package (1 tablespoon)
   powdered gelatin dissolved in ¼ cup hot water

Stir the pistachios in a dry sauté pan or skillet over medium heat
until lightly toasted. Set aside. In a sauté pan or skillet, cook the
onion and shallots in the vegetable oil over moderate heat, stirring,
for 5 minutes, or until the onion is softened. Add the chicken livers,
bay leaves, Armagnac, white wine, red coloring, salt and pepper to
taste. Cook the mixture, stirring occasionally, for 8 minutes until
the livers are just cooked through. Add 1 cup of the cream and
simmer the mixture for 2 minutes. Discard the bay leaves.

Transfer the mixture to a blender or food processor, add the
gelatin sheets or dissolved gelatin, and purée until smooth. Transfer the mixture to a bowl. Place the bowl in a larger bowl of ice
cubes and stir from time to time. Whip the remaining 2 cups of

continued

cream to soft peaks and set aside. Add the pistachios to the liver mixture and stir. Fold the whipped cream into the mixture, season to taste, and transfer it to a serving dish or terrine.

Chill the mousse, covered, for at least 6 hours or overnight. Serve with fresh corn bread or melba toast.

YIELD: ABOUT 5 CUPS

J eremiah Tower is the co-owner and chef of Stars Restaurant in San Francisco and the author of the forthcoming book *New American Classics* (Harper and Row). These recipes were created for *Menus and Music* by Jeremiah, who especially likes the music of Cole Porter.

∧   ∧   ∧   ∧   ∧

MENU

RILLETTES OF SMOKED FISH WITH
GARDEN SALAD AND BITTER GREENS

ICED OYSTERS WITH SPICY LAMB
SAUSAGE

AVOCADO, PINK GRAPEFRUIT, MANGO,
AND MUSHROOM SALAD

RILLETTES OF SMOKED FISH WITH GARDEN SALAD AND BITTER GREENS

The pitfall with *rillettes* of any kind is overgrinding or processing the meat or fish. Mixing in the whipped butter by hand makes a light, fluffy texture. Don't forget that cold food needs more seasoning than hot food.

4 ounces smoked sturgeon

4 ounces smoked trout

4 ounces smoked salmon

4 tablespoons soft unsalted butter

Salt and freshly ground pepper

2 tablespoons clarified butter*

1 small head curly endive

2 small heads red leaf lettuce

2 small heads green leaf lettuce

1 bunch watercress

Juice of 1 lemon

½ cup virgin olive oil

½ cup hazelnut oil

Melba toasts

Skin and bone the fish and break it up by hand. Set aside. Whip the soft butter until fluffy. Add the fish to the butter and mix by hand until incorporated but still slightly coarse. Add salt and pepper to taste. Pack loosely into ramekins and smooth the top. Pour clarified butter about ⅟₁₆ inch thick over the *rillettes*. Cover and refrigerate overnight.

Wash, dry, and chill the salad greens. Mix the lemon juice and salt and pepper to taste together. Whisk in the two oils. Toss with the combined salad greens.

Place each of the ramekin dishes in the center of a cold plate and arrange the salad around the edges. Garnish with melba toasts.

YIELD: 8 FIRST-COURSE SERVINGS

* To make clarified butter, melt butter over low heat. Let the melted butter stand a few minutes, so the milk solids settle. Skim any foam from the top and pour the clear yellow clarified butter through a sieve into a container. Store in the refrigerator.

ICED OYSTERS WITH SPICY LAMB SAUSAGE

For this recipe always use the freshest oysters possible. My favorites are Tomales Bay, Golden Mantels, or Belons. When preparing the sausages it is important to keep the meat grinder, fat, and meat as cold as possible.

3 pounds lamb, well trimmed and chilled

1 pound veal, well trimmed and chilled

1½ pounds pork back fat, chilled

5 *serrano* chilies, seeded and minced

¼ teaspoon cayenne

Minced fresh thyme and marjoram to taste

Salt and freshly ground pepper

1 dozen fresh oysters in their shells

Parsley sprigs

8 lemon wedges

Pass the meats through the grinder once using a medium-sized die. Pass the fat through the grinder twice using a medium-sized die. Set aside in the refrigerator.

Start a charcoal fire or preheat the broiler. Mix the meat and fat mixture with the chilies, cayenne, and herbs. Work quickly but do not overwork, keeping the mixture cold at all times. Add salt and pepper to taste. Grill one patty to test and adjust the seasoning as needed. Shape the mixture into 8 patties ¼ inch thick and 3 inches in diameter.

To prepare the oysters, scrub them clean with a sturdy brush under cold water. Open the oysters at the hinge and free the body from the shell. Reserve the deep half-shells after wiping the edges of any dirt.

Grill the sausage patties approximately 6 minutes. Arrange the oysters on the half-shells. Lay 3 oysters on shaved ice in a cold gratin dish and place the dish on the upper half of the plate. Place 2 grilled lamb sausages on the lower half of the plate. Garnish with a sprig of parsley and 2 lemon wedges.

YIELD: 4 FIRST-COURSE SERVINGS

AVOCADO, PINK GRAPEFRUIT, MANGO, AND MUSHROOM SALAD

12 mushrooms

1 tablespoon minced shallot

Fresh lemon juice to taste

Salt and freshly ground pepper to taste

1 cup olive oil

2 avocados, peeled and sliced

2 mangoes, peeled and sliced

1 pink grapefruit, peeled and sectioned

3 tablespoons balsamic vinegar

Minced fresh tarragon

Fresh tarragon leaves, blanched and drained, or fresh chervil leaves

Slice the mushrooms very thinly. Mix the minced shallot, lemon juice, and salt and pepper. Whisk in ¼ cup of the olive oil. Pour over the mushrooms, toss them and set aside. Fan the avocados out on one side of each of 4 salad plates. Fan out the mango slices and grapefruit sections on the other side. Overlap the mushroom slices in the center. Mix the balsamic vinegar with salt, pepper, and tarragon to taste. Whisk in the remaining ¾ cup olive oil. Pour the dressing over the avocado, mango, and grapefruit. Garnish with blanched tarragon leaves or fresh chervil.

YIELD: 4 FIRST-COURSE SERVINGS

Judith Ets-Hokin

CULINARY COMPANY

J udith Ets-Hokin founded the Judith Ets-Hokin Culinary Company in 1972. She has studied with Paul Meyer and Paul Quiaud in the United States and has certificates from Cordon Bleu in London and from cooking schools in Dieppe, France, and Florence, Italy. She is the author of *The San Francisco Dinner Party Cookbook* and director of The Judith Ets-Hokin Cooking School.

Judith introduces her menu as follows: "This menu is 'easy' in several ways: the entire menu can be prepared well ahead of serving, indeed, some of the dishes need several days to develop their full flavors; it is easy to serve (everything is out on the buffet table before guests arrive), easy to eat (guests don't need a table since food can be eaten with fingers or forks), and easy to decrease amounts or delete dishes for smaller groups or increase recipes for large groups. It is particularly sensuous and delicious with its blend of colors, tastes, and textures."

∧ ∧ ∧ ∧ ∧

MENU

HORS D'OEUVRES

STEAK TARTARE ON TOAST ROUNDS

STEAMED HERBED SHRIMP WITH GREEN MAYONNAISE

STUFFED MUSHROOMS

GRAVLAX ON THIN BLACK BREAD WITH MUSTARD-DILL SAUCE

BUFFET SUPPER

VITELLO TONNATO

BONELESS CHICKEN IN PIMIENTO SAUCE

BROCCOLI TOSSED IN HAZELNUT OIL

FRESH ITALIAN MOZZARELLA WITH TOMATOES, BASIL AND OLIVE OIL

TINY NEW POTATOES WITH HERBS

BAGUETTES WITH FRESH SWEET BUTTER

DESSERT

INDIVIDUAL KIWI-STRAWBERRY TARTS

JUDITH ETS-HOKIN

STEAK TARTARE

1 pound lean beef

1 French-style baguette

Olive oil for sautéing

2 tablespoons chopped onion

1 egg yolk

Dash of Tabasco

1 tablespoon capers, drained

8 anchovy fillets, chopped

1 tablespoon chopped fresh chives

Salt and freshly ground pepper to taste

1 teaspoon Dijon mustard

2 tablespoons cognac

Grind or chop the beef to a medium-fine consistency. Slice the baguette into ¼-inch slices. In a large sauté pan or skillet, heat 2 to 3 tablespoons olive oil and sauté the bread slices in batches until golden brown, adding more oil as needed. Drain the toast on paper towels.

Combine the beef with all the remaining ingredients, making sure everything is well blended. Taste for seasoning. Form into a loaf or a mound on a serving dish. Surround with the toast.

YIELD: 16 SERVINGS

STEAMED HERBED SHRIMP
WITH GREEN MAYONNAISE

Four 12-inch branches fresh rosemary

1 bay leaf

3 garlic cloves

½ onion, chopped

2 cups dry white wine

1 pound large shrimp (16 to 20 per pound)

1 cup virgin olive oil

Green Mayonnaise, following

Combine 3 branches of the rosemary, the bay leaf, garlic, onion, and wine in the bottom portion of a steamer and bring to a boil. Reduce to a simmer.

Peel and devein the shrimp, leaving the tail shell intact. Steam the shrimp 1 minute over the simmering liquid. Remove the shrimp and, while still hot, place in the olive oil. Add ¼ cup of the steaming liquid and the remaining branch of rosemary. Cover and marinate in the refrigerator in a glass or stainless steel bowl. Serve on skewers with Green Mayonnaise.

YIELD: 16 TO 20 HORS D'OEUVRES

GREEN MAYONNAISE

¼ cup watercress leaves

2 teaspoons chopped fresh chives

2 teaspoons fresh tarragon leaves

¼ cup minced fresh parsley

2 teaspoons hot-sweet mustard

1 cup mayonnaise

Mince the watercress, chives, and tarragon. Combine all the ingredients and blend well. Allow to stand for 2 hours before serving.

YIELD: ABOUT 1¼ CUPS

STUFFED MUSHROOMS

24 large mushrooms

¼ cup olive oil

¼ cup minced onion

1 garlic clove, minced

½ cup minced green bell pepper

½ teaspoon salt

½ teaspoon freshly ground pepper

3 tablespoons freshly grated Parmesan

1 tablespoon bread crumbs or more

Preheat the oven to 375°. Clean the mushrooms and remove the stems. Mince the mushroom stems. Heat the olive oil in a sauté pan or skillet and sauté the onion, garlic, green pepper, and mushroom stems 5 minutes. Remove from the heat and mix in the salt, ground pepper, cheese, and bread crumbs. Stuff the mushrooms. Place in an oiled baking dish and bake 15 minutes. Serve at room temperature.

YIELD: 24 HORS D'OEUVRES

GRAVLAX

This Scandinavian dish of cured salmon with dill is made 3 days before serving.

One 2-pound center-cut salmon chunk

1 bunch fresh dill

¼ cup coarse salt

¼ cup sugar

2 tablespoons peppercorns, crushed

1 teaspoon white wine vinegar

Thin slices black bread

Lemon wedges

Freshly ground black pepper

Mustard-Dill Sauce, following

Cut the salmon in half lengthwise and remove the bone. Place half the fish, skin side down, in a deep nonmetal container. Place the bunch of dill on the fish. Sprinkle the salt, sugar, and peppercorns over the dill and moisten with the vinegar. Top with the other half of the fish, skin side up; cover with aluminum foil and place a 2-pound weight on top. Refrigerate 3 days, turning the fish every 12 hours and basting with the liquid marinade that accumulates.

Remove the fish from the marinade, rinse away the seasonings, and pat it dry. Place the separated halves skin side down and slice thinly on the diagonal. Serve with black bread, lemon wedges, freshly ground pepper, and Mustard-Dill Sauce.

YIELD: ABOUT 16 HORS D'OEUVRES

MUSTARD-DILL SAUCE

4 tablespoons Dijon mustard

1 teaspoon dry mustard

3 tablespoons minced fresh dill

3 tablespoons sugar

12 tablespoons white wine vinegar

⅓ cup vegetable oil

Combine the mustards, dill, sugar, and vinegar until well blended. Stirring constantly with a whisk, slowly add the oil until it forms a thick sauce.

YIELD: ABOUT ¾ CUP

VITELLO TONNATO

1 teaspoon salt

1 teaspoon freshly ground pepper

One 3-pound rolled leg of veal

3 tablespoons vegetable oil or more

½ cup sliced onion

1 carrot, sliced

10 fresh parsley sprigs

1 garlic clove

One 7-ounce can tuna in olive oil

10 anchovy fillets

¼ cup fresh lemon juice

⅔ cup virgin olive oil

2 teaspoons capers, drained

Preheat the oven to 375°. Rub the salt and pepper over the surface of the veal. Heat the oil in a Dutch oven and brown the veal on all sides over high heat. Discard any fat and add the onion, carrot, 4 sprigs of the parsley, and the garlic. Place on the stove, turn on the heat to high, and pour enough boiling water over the meat to just cover. As soon as the liquid comes back to the boil, cover the casserole, place in the oven, and cook until barely tender, approximately 1 to 1½ hours. Allow the veal to cool in the liquid.

Purée the tuna, anchovies, and lemon juice in a blender or food processor. Very gradually add the olive oil to the consistency of thin mayonnaise. Slice the veal and arrange on a serving platter, not

continued

JUDITH ETS-HOKIN

overlapping but each slice touching. Spread a little sauce over each slice, then begin another layer. Repeat as necessary, ending with sauce. Sprinkle with capers. Chop the remaining parsley sprigs and sprinkle over the veal. Cover and refrigerate 2 days before serving.

YIELD: 16 SERVINGS

BONELESS CHICKEN IN PIMIENTO SAUCE

6 quarts water

1 carrot

1 celery stalk

1 onion

4 pounds boneless chicken breasts, skin left on

4 tablespoons capers, drained

1 cup virgin olive oil

16 anchovy filets in oil

3 tablespoons flour

4 garlic cloves, minced

4 ounces whole pimiento

Salt and freshly ground pepper to taste

⅔ cup red wine vinegar

Place the water in a soup pot. Add the carrot, celery, and onion and bring to a boil. Boil 5 minutes. Add the chicken breasts. When the water returns to a boil, lower the heat and simmer the breasts 1 minute. Remove from the heat and allow to cool in the broth 10 minutes. Remove the breasts from the liquid. Strain, defat, and reserve the stock. Remove the skin from the breast meat and discard. Cut the chicken into strips and place on a serving dish. Sprinkle the capers over the chicken.

Heat 3 cups of the defatted broth to the boiling point. Heat the oil in a large sauté pan or skillet. When it is hot, add the anchovies, mashing them with a wooden spoon into a paste. Add the flour and stir until the flour is golden brown. Add the boiling broth and stir 2 to 3 minutes more. Add the garlic and half the pimiento and simmer about 10 minutes more. Cool slightly and purée in a blender or food processor. Return the puréed mixture to the pan, taste for salt and pepper, and heat. Add the wine vinegar, combine well, and pour over the chicken.

Cut the remaining pimiento into strips and use to garnish the dish. Cover and marinate in the refrigerator 2 days before serving.

YIELD: 16 SERVINGS

BROCCOLI TOSSED IN HAZELNUT OIL

4 bunches broccoli

1 to 3 tablespoons hazelnut oil

Salt and freshly ground pepper

Cut the broccoli into florets, reserving the stalks for another use. Boil or steam the broccoli until barely tender—do not overcook. Drain and dry on paper towels. While the broccoli is still hot, place it in a bowl and add 1 tablespoon of the hazelnut oil and salt and pepper to taste. Toss well. If the broccoli seems a little dry, add more oil by the teaspoon until the broccoli is lightly coated. Allow to stand 1 hour at room temperature before serving.

YIELD: 16 SERVINGS

FRESH ITALIAN MOZZARELLA WITH TOMATOES, BASIL, AND OLIVE OIL

1 pound fresh Italian mozzarella*

16 slices ripe tomato

Salt and freshly ground pepper to taste

About 10 fresh basil leaves

Virgin olive oil

Slice the mozzarella into 16 slices and alternate with the tomatoes in an overlapping design on a serving platter. Sprinkle lightly with salt and pepper. Cut approximately 10 basil leaves into "ribbons" and sprinkle over the tomatoes and cheese. Drizzle olive oil over all. Allow to stand at room temperature 1 hour before serving.

YIELD: 16 SERVINGS

* If fresh Italian mozzarella is not available, use fresh domestic mozzarella. This dish can only be made with fresh cheese.

TINY NEW POTATOES WITH HERBS

4 pounds tiny red potatoes

¼ cup dry white wine

⅓ cup white wine vinegar

1½ cups virgin olive oil

3 tablespoons chopped shallots

1 tablespoon salt

1 teaspoon ground white pepper

1 bunch fresh parsley sprigs, chopped

6 tablespoons minced fresh dill

4 ounces niçoise olives

Place the unpeeled potatoes in boiling water to cover and cook until tender. Slice or quarter the potatoes while still hot. Heat the wine, wine vinegar, and olive oil. While the potatoes are hot, toss with the shallots, salt, pepper, and hot wine mixture. Add the parsley, dill, and olives. Adjust seasoning.

YIELD: 16 SERVINGS

INDIVIDUAL KIWI-STRAWBERRY TARTS

1 recipe Plain Pastry, following

1 cup milk

¼ cup sugar

1 tablespoon flour

1 tablespoon cornstarch

3 egg yolks

2 teaspoons vanilla extract

1 teaspoon unsalted butter

1 cup heavy cream

5 to 6 ripe kiwi fruits

1 basket strawberries

1 cup wine jelly

Preheat the oven to 375°. Make the pastry, roll it out, and cut it into 16 circles slightly larger than an individual tartlet mold. Ease the circles into each of 16 molds. Cut out 16 rounds of waxed paper, place them on top of the pastry, and fill each tart mold with pie weights or dried beans. Bake until the pastry is lightly browned. Remove the waxed paper and weights from the pastry, take each pastry shell from its mold, and allow to cool before filling.

To make the pastry cream, combine the milk and sugar in a small saucepan. Bring to a boil and remove from the heat. In a bowl, combine the flour, cornstarch, and egg yolks and beat until well mixed. Beat a little of the hot milk into the egg mixture, then add the egg mixture to the pan of milk, beating continually with a whisk until combined. Return to the heat and bring to a boil, whisking constantly. Remove from the heat, add the vanilla, pour into a bowl, and rub the top of the cream with the teaspoon of butter to prevent a skin from forming. Cool completely.

Just before assembling the tarts, whip the heavy cream and fold into the cooled pastry cream. Peel and slice the kiwis. Wash, dry, and slice the strawberries. To assemble: Heat the wine jelly. Spoon the pastry cream into each tartlet, arrange the strawberry and kiwi slices in overlapping designs on top of the pastry cream, and brush with the warm wine jelly.

YIELD: 16 TARTS

PLAIN PASTRY

½ cup (1 stick) plus 1 tablespoon unsalted butter

2 cups all-purpose flour

¼ teaspoon salt

4 tablespoons cold water

With a pastry cutter or 2 knives, cut the butter into the flour and salt until crumbly, or process 10 seconds in a food processor. Sprinkle in the water and mix with a fork, then press together in a ball (or process for 20 seconds in a food processor). Allow the dough to rest in the refrigerator at least 1 hour before rolling out.

YIELD: ONE 9-INCH DOUBLE CRUST OR 16 TART SHELLS

E D I B L E · A R T

Edible Art was created in 1980 by Sharon Polster and Robin McMillan with the view that food is an artistic medium. Their combination of quality ingredients and stylized presentation has served clients worldwide, including Paloma Picasso, the Fine Arts Museums of San Francisco, and the cast of *Dynasty*. The following hors d'oeuvres recipes were prepared by Sharon Polster, who is also the food stylist for the covers of *Menus and Music*.

∧ ∧ ∧ ∧ ∧

MENU

SPINACH CREPE SPIRALS

MU SHU PORK

EADRINOS WITH CHIPOTLE SAUCE

SPINACH CREPE SPIRALS

These are great for either passed hors d'oeuvres or as a buffet dish. They look particularly stunning on Chinese lacquer red. The crepes can be cooked and frozen up to 2 weeks in advance; the filling can be made up to 3 days in advance.

CREPES

1 bunch fresh spinach, stemmed

3 eggs

1½ cups milk

1 cup all-purpose flour

½ teaspoon salt

½ teaspoon ground pepper

1 bunch green onions, minced

Oil for frying

FILLING

1 pound softened cream cheese

1 tablespoon vodka

1 bunch fresh basil, minced, or 1 tablespoon dried basil

Grated zest of 2 lemons

4 garlic cloves, chopped

1 teaspoon ground pepper

3 ounces dehydrated sun-dried tomatoes, chopped

½ cup toasted pine nuts*

To make the crepes, wash the spinach leaves well, mince, and steam until wilted; squeeze dry. In a blender or food processor, combine the eggs, milk, flour, salt, and pepper. Blend for 1½ minutes. Pour into a bowl and whisk in the steamed spinach and green onions. The batter should be the consistency of heavy cream. If it is too thick, thin with ½ tablespoon water. Over medium heat, heat a 10-inch skillet (preferably nonstick), and brush with oil. Pour in approximately ⅓ cup crepe batter. Roll the pan to spread the batter thinly and evenly. Cook until slightly browned and dry; flip over and cook about 30 seconds. Remove from the pan and cool. Repeat until all the batter is used.

To make the filling, combine the cream cheese with all the ingredients except the sun-dried tomatoes and pine nuts. Spread each crepe with a thin layer of the cream cheese mixture. Sprinkle with the sun-dried tomatoes and pine nuts. Roll tightly, wrap in plastic wrap, and chill.

Slice each roll in 8 to 10 slices. Cut on a slight diagonal so the slices are oval rather than round.

YIELD: 32 TO 40 SLICES

* To toast the pine nuts, stir them in a dry skillet over medium heat until golden.

MU SHU PORK

1 quart water

½ cup golden needles * (optional)

¼ cup dried *shiitake* or wood ear mushrooms

1 tablespoon Asian sesame oil

2 eggs

¼ pound ground pork

1 tablespoon minced fresh ginger

3 green onions, minced

½ tablespoon cornstarch mixed with 1 tablespoon dry sherry

⅓ cup *hoisin* sauce

12 *mu shu* wrappers

3 bunches chives

Bring the water to a boil in a large pot and turn off the heat. Add the golden needles and wood ears or *shiitakes*. Cover and let steep 1 hour. Drain and mince. Heat the sesame oil in an omelet pan or small skillet. Beat the eggs and pour them into a skillet with the sesame oil. Cook like an omelet. Remove from the pan, still in circular form, then roll jelly-roll fashion. Cut into ⅛-inch crosswise strips. Reserve.

In a sauté pan or skillet, sauté the pork. Drain off all but a little fat. Add the ginger, green onions, golden needles, and mushrooms; cook 5 minutes. Add the cornstarch mixture and cook 5 minutes longer. Add the omelet strips and *hoisin* sauce and mix well.

Cut the 12 *mu shu* wrappers into 4 squares. Dip the chives into boiling water and place on paper towels. Place 2 teaspoons of filling in one corner of each wrapper. Fold the right and left corners over this. Roll into a spiral and tie with a chive. Place the wrappers in a steamer basket over boiling water and steam about 3 minutes.

YIELD: 48 HORS D'OEUVRES

* Golden needles, or dried lily flower buds, can be found in Asian markets.

EADRINOS WITH CHIPOTLE SAUCE

2 pounds Monterey jack cheese

One 3-ounce can sliced peeled green chilies

4 *serrano* chilies, minced

5 garlic cloves

3 bunches fresh cilantro, chopped

2 tablespoons ground cumin

Dash cayenne pepper

½ package (50) wonton wrappers

2 egg yolks slightly beaten with 1 tablespoon water

Oil for deep-frying

Chipotle Sauce, following

Shred the cheese and mix in both kinds of chilies, garlic, cilantro, cumin, and cayenne. Brush the edges of each wonton wrapper with the egg-water mixture. Place about 2 teaspoons of the cheese mixture in the center of each wrapper and bring the corners and edges up into a star shape, sealing and pinching as you go. Place on a tray and freeze for several hours or up to 1 month. Heat the oil to 350°, drop in the *eadrinos*, and fry until golden. Drain on paper towels and serve immediately with Chipotle Sauce.

YIELD: 50 HORS D'OEUVRES

CHIPOTLE SAUCE

2 cups sour cream

½ cup red salsa (your own or bottled kind)

1 bunch fresh cilantro, chopped

Good dash Tabasco sauce

Mix all the ingredients together. Feel free to make the sauce hotter with cayenne pepper.

YIELD: 2½ CUPS

NARSAI'S

Narsai David is the owner of Narsai's Catering and Narsai's at I. Magnin as well as the host on KCBS radio of "Narsai and Company" and the "KCBS Saturday Kitchen." He has been a television chef and nutrition counselor, and Narsai's Restaurant, which he closed in 1985, was a perennial Holiday Award Winner that was awarded a place on the *New York Times*'s Ten Finest Wine Lists. Narsai David is the author of the forthcoming book, *Monday Night at Narsai's* (Simon and Schuster).

∧ ∧ ∧ ∧ ∧

MENU

GRAVLAX

DUCK LIVER PATE

PORT WINE ASPIC

GRAVLAX

Gravlax is a traditional Scandinavian dish of salmon cured with dill, salt, pepper, and sugar.

1 teaspoon dried dill weed, or 1 tablespoon minced fresh dill

1 teaspoon dill seed

2 pounds salmon fillet with skin

2 tablespoons salt

¼ cup sugar

¼ teaspoon freshly ground black pepper

¼ teaspoon ground allspice

¼ cup Aquavit

½ cup heavy cream

Coarse-ground mustard to taste

Thin slices dark rye bread

Mix the dill weed and seeds and sprinkle half of this mixture in the bottom of a flat dish that the salmon almost fills. Slash the skin side of the salmon with a sharp knife. Place the salmon skin-side down in the dish and sprinkle with the remaining dill. Blend the salt, sugar, pepper, and allspice. Distribute this mixture evenly over the salmon and pat lightly into the flesh. Pour the Aquavit over the fish.

Cover the dish with plastic wrap and place a 2-pound weight on top of it to weigh the fish down evenly. Refrigerate at least 2 days, spooning juices over the fish occasionally during this time. After a day remove the weight. The salmon will keep as long as 5 days in its brine, but it gradually grows too salty.

Slice the fish thinly across the grain on a diagonal to the skin. Cut away from the skin. Whip the cream and fold the mustard into it. Serve the salmon with the whipped cream mixture alongside, accompanied with dark rye.

YIELD: 8 TO 12 FIRST-COURSE SERVINGS

DUCK LIVER PATE

1 cup sliced onion

1¼ cups (2½ sticks) butter

1 green apple, peeled and thinly sliced

1 pound duck livers

¼ cup dry sherry or applejack

¼ cup heavy cream

1¼ teaspoons salt

1 teaspoon fresh lemon juice

Port Wine Aspic, following, or iced butter cut-outs and parsley sprigs

In a sauté pan or skillet, sauté the onion in ½ cup (1 stick) of the butter until it starts to brown nicely. Add the apple and cook 3 to 4 minutes until the apple starts to soften. Add the duck livers and sauté over high heat until they are pink. Transfer this mixture to a blender. Soften the pan residue with the sherry or applejack, add it

continued

to the blender with the cream, and blend. Remove this mixture from the blender and cool to lukewarm. Beat the remaining ¾ cup of the butter until soft and slowly add the liver paste. Add the salt and lemon juice. Pack into a terrine. Pour the Port Wine Aspic through a strainer over the terrine to make a layer ⅛ inch to ¼ inch thick; chill until set. Or, if you prefer, decorate the pâté with iced butter cut-outs and parsley. Serve chilled, in the terrine.

YIELD: ONE 2-POUND TERRINE

PORT WINE ASPIC

2 teaspoons plain gelatin

1 cup port

2 tablespoons sugar

1 tablespoon water

3 tablespoons red wine vinegar

½ teaspoon dried tarragon

Soften the gelatin in ¼ cup of the port. Set aside. In a saucepan, dissolve the sugar in the water. Cook rapidly until the sugar melts and reaches a medium-dark caramel color. Add the vinegar and the remaining ¾ cup port, and crumble in the tarragon. Simmer for 2 minutes. Add the gelatin to the hot mixture and stir until dissolved.

YIELD: ABOUT 1¼ CUPS

PARTIES, PARTIES, PARTIES.

Parties, Parties, Parties was founded in 1978 by Donna Balsamo because she wanted to create celebrations featuring the finest cuisine combined with theatrical excitement. A favorite setting of hers for a posh cocktail party accompanied by the music of Cole Porter, George Gershwin, and Duke Ellington is a beautiful San Francisco Pacific Heights mansion built by James Flood, a Comstock baron, at the turn of the century. This menu was prepared for Parties, Parties, Parties by Betsy Ayers and Marty Rosenblum.

MENU

CHAMPAGNE-MUSTARD PRAWNS
BRUT CHAMPAGNE

SCALLOP CEVICHE ON ENDIVE

FIVE-SPICED CHICKEN

STEAMED SNOW PEAS WITH JALAPENO-
CREAM DIPPING SAUCE
DRY GEWÜRZTRAMINER

SHERRIED MUSHROOM CAPS

FRESH PEARS WITH WALNUT
GORGONZOLA CREAM
MERLOT

CHAMPAGNE-MUSTARD PRAWNS

½ cup olive oil

2 teaspoons minced shallots

1 tablespoon minced fresh chives

2 pounds large prawns (16 to 20 per pound), peeled and deveined

¾ cup dry champagne

1 tablespoon butter

2 tablespoons Mendocino mustard or other hot-sweet mustard

Juice of 1 lemon

Fresh-ground pepper

Heat the olive oil in a sauté pan or skillet and sauté the shallots and chives for 1 minute. Add the prawns and sauté 30 seconds on each side or until they turn pink. Add the champagne and bring to a boil (to cook out the alcohol). Turn off the heat and blend in the butter, mustard, and lemon juice. Sprinkle with fresh-ground pepper and serve with sandwich picks.

YIELD: 32 TO 40 HORS D'OEUVRES

SCALLOP CEVICHE ON ENDIVE

2 pounds bay scallops

1 large Bermuda onion, finely diced

½ cup chopped canned green chilies

1 cup diced tomatoes

2 garlic cloves, minced

1½ cups fresh squeezed lime juice

½ cup fresh cilantro leaves, minced

4 heads endive, trimmed, cleaned, and separated into leaves

Rinse the scallops under cool water and drain. Mix all the ingredients except the endive together in a glass or stainless steel bowl. Mix well and cover. Marinate in the refrigerator for 4 to 6 hours.

Place the endive leaves on a tray, spoon the ceviche into the leaves, and serve.

YIELD: HORS D'OEUVRES FOR 16 PEOPLE

FIVE-SPICED CHICKEN

The five-spice powder, Asian sesame oil, and hot chili oil are all available in Asian markets.

MARINADE

½ cup peanut oil

½ cup tamari or soy sauce

½ cup sake or dry sherry

½ cup Mendocino mustard or other hot-sweet mustard

4 garlic cloves

2 tablespoons five-spice powder

2 tablespoons Asian sesame oil

1 tablespoon hot chili oil

3 pounds chicken breasts, boned, skinned, and cut into 1-inch cubes

Blend all the marinade ingredients in a blender until well mixed. Place the chicken in a glass or stainless steel bowl and mix with the marinade. Cover and refrigerate for 2 or 3 hours. Remove from refrigerator 30 minutes before cooking.

Preheat the broiler. Place the chicken pieces on a sheet pan and cook under the broiler for 2 or 3 minutes. Serve on small skewers or sandwich picks.

YIELD: HORS D'OEUVRES FOR 16 PEOPLE

STEAMED SNOW PEAS WITH JALAPENO-CREAM DIPPING SAUCE

DIPPING SAUCE

4 ounces cream cheese, softened

1 teaspoon minced garlic

1 teaspoon minced fresh chives

1 teaspoon minced fresh cilantro

¼ cup heavy cream

¼ cup *jalapeño* jelly

Juice of ½ lime

32 snow peas

Mix the cream cheese with the other sauce ingredients. Steam the snow peas for about 1 minute, so they are still crispy. Place the *jalapeño* cream in a bowl with the snow peas arranged around the bowl.

YIELD: HORS D'OEUVRES FOR 16 PEOPLE

SHERRIED MUSHROOMS CAPS

¼ cup olive oil

4 tablespoons unsalted butter

3 garlic cloves, minced

32 mushroom caps (half-dollar size)

continued

1 cup dry sherry

2 tablespoons minced fresh chives

Juice of 1 lemon

Salt and pepper to taste

Heat the oil and butter in a large sauté pan or skillet. Sauté the garlic and mushrooms for about 5 minutes or until golden. Add the sherry and bring to a boil. Stir and cook for another 2 or 3 minutes, until the mushrooms are tender. Add the chives, lemon juice, and salt and pepper to taste. Remove the mushrooms with a slotted spoon and serve warm with toothpicks.

YIELD: 16 SERVINGS

FRESH PEARS WITH WALNUT GORGONZOLA CREAM

⅔ cup walnuts

12 ounces Italian Gorgonzola

⅓ cup heavy cream

8 fresh pears

Stir the walnuts in a dry sauté pan or skillet over medium heat until lightly toasted. Purée the Gorgonzola, cream, and walnuts in a blender or food processor for about 1 minute, or until well mixed. Slice the pears into quarter sections, then peel and core. Put about 1 teaspoon of Gorgonzola cream on top of each section. Serve immediately.

YIELD: 32 HORS D'OEUVRES

taste

Timothy Maxon, creator of Taste, views food at its best as an evolving art form. He combines superb cuisine and visually beautiful presentations in his work. The following menu and recipes for a cocktail party with music by Cole Porter, George Gershwin, and Duke Ellington were created at Taste by Ted Smith.

∧ ∧ ∧ ∧ ∧

MENU

CRAB CAKES WITH RED REMOULADE
SAUCE

FEUILLETE WITH QUAIL EGGS

BETTE DAVIS EYES

GINGER PRAWNS

FILET WITH SNOW PEAS AND MUSTARD-
CAPER SAUCE

MINI-B'STILLA

DRINKS

LE JAZZ HOT
COOL JAZZ
PIANO MAN
THE LADY IN RED

CRAB CAKES

1 red bell pepper, chopped

1 yellow onion, minced

1 celery stalk, chopped

3 tablespoons butter

2 tablespoons all-purpose flour

1 teaspoon Old Bay Seasoning

½ teaspoon Tabasco

1 teaspoon Worcestershire sauce

¼ cup fresh lemon juice

1 to 2 garlic cloves, minced

2 egg yolks

¾ cup heavy cream

1 cup bread crumbs

1 pound fresh cooked crab meat

Cornmeal

Oil for deep-frying

Red Remoulade Sauce, following

Char the pepper evenly all over under a broiler or over a gas flame. Place in a closed paper bag for 15 minutes. Rub off the blackened skin. Remove the stem, seeds, and veins. Coarsely chop the pepper.

In a sauté pan or skillet, sauté the onion and celery in the butter until softened. Add half of the red pepper (reserve half for the Red Remoulade Sauce), flour, seasoning, Tabasco, Worcestershire, lemon juice, and garlic and sauté another 5 to 7 minutes until the flour begins to brown. Beat the egg yolks with the cream and stir into the vegetable mixture. Stir until thickened (the mixture will come away from the sides of the pan). Cool slightly. Add the bread crumbs and crab meat and mix well.

Form with your fingers into coins about 1 inch in diameter and about ½ inch thick. Roll in cornmeal and set aside on waxed paper. Heat the oil in a deep pan to 350° and deep-fry the cakes about 5 minutes or until golden brown. Serve warm with Red Remoulade Sauce.

YIELD: 50 TO 60 HORS D'OEUVRES

RED REMOULADE SAUCE

1 tablespoon prepared horseradish

1 tablespoon capers, drained

½ peeled, seeded, deveined, and chopped red bell pepper (see
    preceding recipe)

1 cup mayonnaise

1 to 2 green onions

1 tablespoon grated lemon zest

¼ cup minced *cornichons*

1 tablespoon minced *jalapeño* chili

¼ cup chopped fresh parsley

Squeeze the horseradish in cheesecloth to get rid of the vinegar. Chop the capers lightly. Mix all the ingredients together in a mixing bowl for a chunky sauce; purée in a blender or food processor for a smoother sauce.

YIELD: 2 CUPS

FEUILLETE WITH QUAIL EGGS

1 sheet frozen puff pastry, thawed

13 quail eggs

Chive Mousseline, following

Zest of 1 lime, cut into very thin slivers

½ bunch fresh dill

2 tablespoons California golden caviar

Preheat the oven to 450°. Cut the puff pastry into medium-sized (1½ inches in diameter) flower shapes. Score an inner ring in each puff pastry with a smaller cutter. Bake about 15 minutes or until golden brown. Remove the scored centers and set the puffs aside.

When ready to serve, cut the quail eggs into quarters. Fill a pastry bag with the *mousseline* and pipe about 1 teaspoon into each puff. Place a quarter egg yolk-side up at an angle in the *mousseline*, cross the egg with a sliver of zest, and place a small sprig of dill at the base of the zest. Place a dollop of caviar on the opposite side of the egg.

Place the quail eggs in a pan of cold water and bring to a simmer for 1½ minutes. Plunge into cold water to cool. Peel the eggs and set aside.

YIELD: 50 HORS D'OEUVRES

CHIVE MOUSSELINE

Other delicious *mousselines* can be made by varying the herbs.

1½ cups *crème fraîche*, following
½ cup mayonnaise
½ bunch fresh chives, minced
Kosher salt to taste
Black pepper to taste

Whip the *crème fraîche* until stiff. Fold in the remaining ingredients.

YIELD: 2 CUPS

CREME FRAICHE

This is much better than sour cream and is also excellent as a topping for fresh fruits and/or pound cake.

1½ cups heavy cream
3 tablespoons buttermilk

Combine the cream and buttermilk in a glass container, cover, and let sit in a fairly warm place (70 to 80°) overnight, then chill. The cream will thicken.

YIELD: 1½ CUPS

BETTE DAVIS EYES

4 ounces Montrachet or similar French goat cheese

25 seedless grapes

½ cup pistachios, ground

Pack the goat cheese around each grape and roll it in the palm of your hand till smooth and round. Refrigerate. Before serving, roll the grapes in the ground pistachios and cut in half.

YIELD: 50 HORS D'OEUVRES

GINGER PRAWNS

½ pound fresh ginger

½ cup (1 stick) unsalted butter

2½ pounds medium shrimp (20 to 25 per pound), cleaned, shelled, and deveined

¼ cup minced garlic

¼ cup fresh lemon juice

1 cup dry white wine

¼ cup chopped fresh parsley

Grate the ginger in a blender or food processor, then purée it. Place the ginger in a clean white towel or cloth and squeeze out as much juice as you can. Discard the pulp.

Melt 2 tablespoons of the butter in a large heavy sauté pan or skillet, then add 12 to 15 of the prawns (one-fourth of the total amount). When the prawns turn pink and opaque, remove them from the pan with a slotted spoon and set them aside. Repeat three times, using the same amount of prawns each time, and adding more butter as necessary. After removing the last batch of prawns, melt the remaining butter in the pan and sauté the garlic until translucent. Add the ginger and lemon juices and the wine. Reduce to a syrupy glaze by boiling. Return the prawns to the pan and toss well in the glaze. Stir in the parsley and serve.

YIELD: 50 TO 60 PRAWNS

FILET WITH SNOW PEAS

One 2½ pound beef tenderloin (filet mignon, in one piece)

1 tablespoon cracked black pepper

1 tablespoon walnut oil

1 tablespoon good bourbon

¼ pound snow peas

Mustard-Caper Sauce, following

Preheat the oven to 425°. Trim the filet of any fat and tie it closed with cotton string. Roll the meat in the cracked pepper. Heat the oil in a heavy sauté pan or skillet. Add the filet and brown on all sides. Pour the bourbon into the pan and light with a match. After the alcohol burns off, remove the filet to a roasting pan and roast until medium rare, approximately 20 minutes. Let cool and slice as thinly as possible.

continued

Cook the snow peas in a large amount of boiling salted water for 1 minute, then drain and plunge into cold water. Drain the peas again, remove the strings and ends, and split the peas in half.

Wrap a bite-sized piece of filet in half a snow pea and close with a toothpick. Serve with Mustard-Caper Sauce.

YIELD: ABOUT 50 HORS D'OEUVRES

MUSTARD-CAPER SAUCE

4 egg yolks

3 tablespoons Dijon mustard

2 teaspoons fresh lemon juice

⅓ bunch fresh chives, snipped

½ cup olive oil

½ cup heavy cream

2 tablespoons capers, drained

Salt and pepper to taste

Put the yolks in a blender or food processor with the mustard, lemon juice, and chives and blend. Add the oil in a thin steady stream with the machine running. Stop and scrape down the sides. Add the cream the same way. Add the capers and blend slightly. Season to taste.

YIELD: 2 CUPS

MINI-B'STILLA

This dish can be prepared and frozen up to 2 weeks in advance.

One 3-pound fryer, cut into quarters

½ cup (1 stick) unsalted butter

Whole unpeeled cloves from ¼ head garlic

¼ bunch fresh parsley

1 red onion, coarsely chopped

½ teaspoon saffron, or to taste

¼ teaspoon ground turmeric

1 teaspoon ground black pepper

1½ teaspoons chopped fresh ginger

1 cinnamon stick

2 eggs

Salt

Lemon juice

Ground cinnamon

½ cup blanched slivered almonds

1 pound *filo* leaves

2 cups (4 sticks) unsalted butter, melted

Powdered sugar

Put the chicken in a large stockpot with the butter, garlic, parsley, onion, saffron, turmeric, pepper, ginger, and cinnamon stick. Cover with water and bring to a slow simmer. Simmer until the meat falls from the bones. Strain and reserve the stock. Remove the chicken meat from the bones and set aside.

continued

Return the stock to the stove and reduce to one-quarter volume. Beat the eggs and stir into ½ cup of the stock. Add this mixture to the stock and stir constantly over low heat until you have an egg-thickened sauce with which to moisten the chicken. Add the sauce to the chicken and reseason with salt, lemon juice, and ground cinnamon to taste. Stir the almonds in a dry sauté pan or skillet over medium heat until they are lightly toasted. Chop the almonds, and add them to the chicken mixture.

To assemble, cut each pound of *filo* into 5 equal parts so that each strip is approximately 1¼ to 1½ inches wide (trim the ends of the roll first). Working quickly and using only 3 or 4 strips at a time, lay the strips flat on a board and brush with the melted butter. Put about a teaspoon of filling on the lower end of each strip and fold like a flag by folding alternate ends over in triangles. Arrange the finished triangles on a sheet pan and brush once more with melted butter. While working, keep the remaining *filo* covered, preferably with a slightly moist towel. Wrap well and chill. The triangles may also be frozen at this point until ready to use.

When ready to serve, place in a preheated 350° oven for about 15 minutes or until golden brown. Let cool a bit before serving; they will stay warm a long time. Serve warm, sprinkled with a little powdered sugar.

YIELD: 100 HORS D'OEUVRES

LE JAZZ HOT

4 ounces light red wine

½ ounce cinnamon schnapps

Thin strip of orange zest

Cinnamon stick

Pour the red wine over ice in a tall glass. Float the schnapps. Garnish with the orange zest and cinnamon stick.

YIELD: 1 DRINK

COOL JAZZ

4 ounces dry white wine

½ ounce Midori (melon liqueur)

Pour the wine over ice in a large wineglass and float the Midori.

YIELD: 1 DRINK

PIANO MAN

2 ounces cognac

½ ounce Galliano

½ ounce Amaretto

Thin strip of lemon zest

Pour the cognac over ice in a rocks glass. Float the two liqueurs. Serve with the lemon zest.

YIELD: 1 DRINK

THE LADY IN RED

2 ounces Bloody Mary mix

½ ounce fresh lemon juice

One bottle premium light lager

Shake of salt

In a glass beer mug, pour the mix and lemon juice, then pour the beer over and salt it.

YIELD: 1 DRINK

Van Wyk Associates

Van Wyk Associates has planned and produced events in northern California for ten years. In recent years, Nancy Van Wyk has orchestrated large corporate receptions in five additional cities. The menus that were presented at these events incorporate the culinary influences and the indigenous ingredients of each American region.

Culinary designer Timothy Levens has created the following reception menu to celebrate the music produced by American composers in the 1930s. As a native Californian, Tim has always been exposed to the influx of cultures and the vast selection of available ingredients which encourage creative California chefs to contribute to the evolving style of American regional cuisine.

∧ ∧ ∧ ∧ ∧

MENU

GRILLED ZUCCHINI AND SUN-DRIED
TOMATOES

PRAWNS ONTIVEROS

BROCCOLI PUREE WITH FIRE-ROASTED
YELLOW PEPPERS

LEMON CRAB TAMALES

CHEVRE AND PISTACHIOS WRAPPED IN
FILO

MINIATURE APRICOT TEA MOUSSE
BASKETS WITH RASPBERRIES

DRINKS

STRAWBERRY COINTREAU MARGARITA
ANAHEIM CHILI BLOODY MARY

GRILLED ZUCCHINI AND SUN-DRIED TOMATOES

1½ pounds zucchini, cut lengthwise into ¼-inch-thick slices

VINAIGRETTE

Juice of 3 limes

¼ cup extra-virgin olive oil

Salt and white pepper to taste

One 8-ounce jar sun-dried tomatoes in oil

Place the zucchini slices on a hot grill. Blacken on one side (3 to 5 minutes). Remove. Mix together the vinaigrette ingredients and pour into a nonmetal container over the warm zucchini. Marinate for 20 minutes. Cut the sun-dried tomatoes into ¼-inch pieces. Place the zucchini cooked-side down, place the tomato on top, roll up, and keep in place with a toothpick.

YIELD: 40 HORS D'OEUVRES

PRAWNS ONTIVEROS

1 bottle Corona or other Mexican beer

1 tablespoon Asian sesame oil

3 *jalapeño* chilies, seeded and minced (or use chili sesame oil)

¼ cup coriander seeds

2 pounds large shrimp, shelled and deveined

1 bunch fresh cilantro, chopped

In a nonmetal container, mix together the beer, sesame oil, chilies, and coriander seeds. Marinate the shrimp in the refrigerator overnight. Drain off the beer, leaving the coriander seeds. Grill the shrimp over mesquite charcoal until they turn pink, 2 to 3 minutes. Sprinkle with chopped cilantro and serve hot.

YIELD: 40 PRAWNS

BROCCOLI PUREE WITH FIRE-ROASTED YELLOW PEPPERS

1 large head broccoli

2 small garlic cloves

¼ to ⅓ cup virgin olive oil

Salt and pepper to taste

2 large yellow bell peppers

Toast points or rounds

Wash the broccoli. Cut off the large stems and discard. Blanch the broccoli in boiling water for 30 seconds. Remove and cool in ice water. Drain well.

Mince the garlic in a blender or food processor. Add the broccoli and purée. Slowly pour in the olive oil. Mix until blended. Taste for salt and pepper. Chill. Roast the yellow peppers under a broiler or over an open flame until blackened all over. Remove and place in a tightly closed paper bag. When cool, remove the skin and seeds. Slice into strips. Spread the broccoli purée on toast and garnish with sliced yellow pepper.

YIELD: 40 HORS D'OEUVRES

LEMON CRAB TAMALES

Masa harina is a corn flour available in Latino markets and some large supermarkets.

TAMALE DOUGH

4 dozen dried cornhusks

⅓ cup lard or vegetable shortening

2 cups *masa harina*

1½ teaspoons salt

1½ teaspoons baking powder

1½ cups warm chicken broth

2 teaspoons grated lemon zest

FILLING

2½ pounds fresh cooked crab meat (preferably whole leg meat)

¼ cup minced green onions

2 bunches fresh cilantro (leaves only)

1 large carrot, cut into 48 strips 2 inches long

To make the tamale dough, soak the cornhusks in hot water to cover for 2 hours. Set aside. Cream the lard. Mix together the *masa*, salt, and baking powder. Add to the lard slowly and mix until incorporated. Slowly add the warm broth to make a slightly moist dough. Stir in the lemon zest.

Drain the cornhusks. Spread 1 tablespoon of dough onto each cornhusk. Add 2 teaspoons crabmeat, ¼ teaspoon green onion, 2 or 3 cilantro leaves, and 1 carrot strip. Roll and hold tight. Place in a steamer over boiling water. Cook 30 to 45 minutes, or until the dough is firm. Serve with fresh salsa.

YIELD: 48 TAMALES

CHEVRE AND PISTACHIOS WRAPPED IN FILO

1 cup pistachios, ground not powdered

½ cup *chèvre*

2 ounces ricotta cheese

Salt and white pepper to taste

2 sheets (14 by 18 inches) fresh or thawed frozen *filo* pastry

Melted butter or olive oil

Preheat the oven to 375°. Mix together the pistachios, *chèvre*, ricotta, and salt and pepper. Place the 2 sheets of *filo* , with the 14-inch length on the sides, on a large cutting surface. Brush the top sheet with melted butter. Cut into 2-inch-wide strips. Place ½ teaspoon of the *chèvre*-pistachio mixture onto each strip of *filo*. Fold by alternate corners into triangles. Brush the tops with butter or oil and bake until golden brown, 5 to 10 minutes. Cool slightly and serve.

YIELD: 40 TO 50 HORS D'OEUVRES

VAN WYK ASSOCIATES

MINIATURE APRICOT TEA MOUSSE BASKETS WITH RASPBERRIES

MERINGUE BASKETS

Dash of salt

4 egg whites

1 cup superfine sugar

APRICOT TEA MOUSSE

¾ cup water

1 tablespoon apricot tea

6 egg yolks, lightly beaten

½ cup sugar

1 pint heavy cream

Grated zest of 1 lemon

1 basket each golden, black, and red raspberries, or any berry or
   combination of berries of your choice

Small dark-chocolate leaves (optional)

To make the baskets, add the salt to the egg whites and beat at
medium-high speed. When the egg whites begin to hold soft peaks,
slowly add ¾ cup of the sugar and continue beating until stiff, then
add the remaining ¼ cup sugar and beat until mixed. Preheat the
oven to 200°. Line baking sheets with parchment or oiled brown
paper and fill a pastry bag with the meringue. Using a small star
tip, pipe bases surrounded by double rings, to make 2-inch-
diameter meringue baskets. Bake until dry (approximately 1 to 1¾

hours). They should be well dried and the color of straw. Store in an airtight container until ready for use.

In a glass jar, place the water and apricot tea. Leave in direct sunlight for 2 days. Strain. In a saucepan over boiling water, combine the egg yolks, sugar, and strained tea. Cook the mixture over boiling water, stirring, until it coats the spoon. Remove from the heat and cool over ice. Whip the cream until stiff and fold in the lemon zest and the cooked custard. Place in a bowl and freeze for 2 hours or overnight. With a small scoop, fill each meringue basket with the mousse. Place 1 or 2 berries on top of the mousse. Garnish with chocolate leaves.

YIELD: 40 BASKETS

STRAWBERRY COINTREAU MARGARITA

Two baskets ripe strawberries, washed, dried, and stemmed

One 750-ml. bottle cointreau

2 ounces white tequila

Juice of 1 lime

To make the strawberry cointreau, place the strawberries in an airtight nonmetal container and pour the cointreau over them. Marinate for at least 2 weeks. Strain through cheesecloth. Store in a sterile container until ready to use.

Rub a glass with lime. Shake ½ ounce of the strawberry cointreau, the tequila and lime juice with crushed ice and strain into the prepared glass.

YIELD: 1 BOTTLE STRAWBERRY COINTREAU; 1 DRINK

ANAHEIM CHILI BLOODY MARY

2½ ounces vodka or white tequila

One Anaheim chili, seeded and deveined

6 ounces tomato juice

1 teaspoon Worcestershire sauce

Celery salt

1 dash Tabasco

1 teaspoon fresh lemon juice

½ teaspoon prepared horseradish

Lime wedge

Celery stalk with leaves

Put all the ingredients except the lime wedge and celery stalk into a blender and mix well. Pour over ice. Garnish with the lime wedge and celery stalk.

YIELD: 1 DRINK

HOTEL
San Francisco

The property atop Nob Hill on which the Fairmont Hotel stands today was originally purchased by Senator James Fair of Virginia City, whose vast wealth in silver earned him the name "Bonanza Jim." Upon the senator's death in 1894, the property passed to his children, and one of his daughters, Theresa Oelrichs, realized the dream to open the Fairmont Hotel in 1907. A magnificent civic banquet was held to open the hotel, which has since hosted many of the city's most splendid social events.

The Oelrichs family relinquished title to the hotel in 1924 and, after a succession of owners, it was purchased in 1945 by its present owner Benjamin Swig and his partner J.D. Weiler. In 1961 a twenty-two-story tower was added, and the Fairmont Hotel and Tower now offers seven hundred guest rooms, eight restaurants and cocktail lounges, twenty-four rooms for banquets and conventions, two orchestras for dancing, and international supper club talent.

∧ ∧ ∧ ∧ ∧

MENU

CHEESE FRITTERS

CRAB MEAT QUICHE

DOMINOES

PRAWN-TARTARE CANAPES

HAWAIIAN HAM ROLLS

VEAL TOURNEDOS ELYSEE WITH
MADEIRA ASPIC

CHEESE FRITTERS

SAUCE

2 cups plain yogurt

¼ teaspoon salt

Pinch celery salt

¼ teaspoon ground white pepper

Generous pinch ground ginger

¼ cup chopped fresh mixed herbs (parsley, chives, dill, a little
rosemary and sage), or 2 teaspoons dried mixed herbs

12 ounces aged Gouda or Cheddar cheese

5 ounces thin bacon slices

2 eggs

¼ cup all-purpose flour

½ cup dried bread crumbs

Oil for deep-frying

Combine the sauce ingredients; blend well and set aside. Cut the
cheese into 1-inch cubes. Wrap each cube in half a bacon slice.
Secure with a wooden pick. In a small bowl, beat the eggs. Spread
the flour in a pie plate. Spread the bread crumbs in a second pie
plate. Roll the cheese and bacon cubes in the eggs, then in the
flour, then in the bread crumbs. Pour oil in a deep heavy skillet to a
1½-inch depth. Heat the oil to 350°. Fry the cubes 4 to 6 minutes or
until golden brown. Serve immediately, along with the sauce.

YIELD: ABOUT 12 HORS D'OEUVRES

CRAB MEAT QUICHE

1 recipe Plain Pastry, page 93

2 pounds fresh cooked crab meat

2 cups grated Swiss cheese

6 eggs

½ cup dry sherry

Salt and cayenne

¾ teaspoon ground nutmeg

3 cups milk

Preheat the oven to 400°. Prepare the pastry recipe. Divide the dough into two halves and roll each out to fit a 9-inch pie pan. Fit into the pans and crimp the edges of the pastry. In a large mixing bowl, mix the crab meat and cheese. Blend well and set aside. In another large bowl, combine all the remaining ingredients and mix well. Season to taste. Divide the crab and cheese mixture equally into each pie. Pour the liquid mixture over the crab and cheese, dividing it equally between the pies. Bake for 15 minutes. Reduce the oven temperature to 325° and bake 20 minutes more.

YIELD: 16 SLICES

DOMINOES

1 hard-cooked egg

6 ounces softened cream cheese

¼ cup heavy cream

½ teaspoon salt

Pinch ground white pepper

1 teaspoon hot prepared mustard

Generous pinch saffron, if desired

½ teaspoon tomato paste

¼ teaspoon paprika

Few drops lemon juice

Pinch sugar

1 tablespoon chopped fresh mixed herbs, or 1 teaspoon dried mixed
 herbs

5 slices pumpernickel bread

Remove the yolk from the egg; reserve the white for another use. In a small bowl, beat together the cream cheese, cream, and salt until creamy. Divide into 4 equal portions. Stir the white pepper and mustard into one portion. Press the egg yolk through a sieve, and stir the egg yolk and saffron, if desired, into one portion. Stir the tomato paste and paprika into one portion. Stir the lemon juice, sugar, and herbs into one portion.

Spread 4 pumpernickel slices alternately with the four flavors of cheese mixture. Stack the pumpernickel slices neatly, one above the other. Top with a fifth slice of pumpernickel. Place a flat plate on top of the bread to prevent the edges from curling. Refrigerate 1 hour or more. To serve, cut the bread into 8 squares or rectangles with a sharp knife.

YIELD: 8 HORS D'OEUVRES

PRAWN-TARTARE CANAPES

1 bunch fresh dill

2 shallots

½ pound medium shrimp, peeled, deveined, and cooked

1 to 2 tablespoons olive oil

1 to 2 teaspoons fresh lemon juice

Generous pinch each salt and white pepper

4 slices pumpernickel bread

1 tablespoon soft butter

1 lemon

Chop the fresh dill, reserving 8 small sprigs. Mince the shallots and shrimp. In a medium bowl, combine the shrimp, shallots, dill, oil, lemon juice, and salt and pepper. Cut the pumpernickel slices in half lengthwise. Spread a little butter on each slice. Spread the shrimp mixture on the bread. Cut 8 thin slices from the center of the lemon. Garnish each canapé with a lemon slice and dill sprig.

Variation: You can also spread the shrimp mixture on toasted white-bread rounds. Garnish with lumpfish caviar.

YIELD: 8 CANAPÉS

HAWAIIAN HAM ROLLS

¼ cup mayonnaise

3 tablespoons farmer's cheese or ricotta cheese

2 teaspoons wine vinegar

¼ teaspoon salt

¼ teaspoon ground white pepper

¼ teaspoon sugar

2 fresh or canned pineapple rings

3 hard-cooked eggs, minced

4 thin 4-inch-square ham slices, trimmed of fat

1 tablespoon soft butter

2 slices dark rye bread, cut into quarters and crusts trimmed

1 tomato, cut into 8 wedges and seeded

Parsley sprigs

Lettuce leaves

In a small bowl, cream together the mayonnaise, cheese, vinegar, salt, pepper, and sugar. Cut the pineapple rings into small pieces. Add the pineapple and eggs to the mayonnaise mixture. Cut each ham slice in half. Spoon an equal amount of mayonnaise mixture on each half-slice of ham. Roll the ham slices. Lightly butter the bread. Place 1 ham roll on each piece of bread. Garnish each ham roll with a tomato wedge and a parsley sprig. Serve on lettuce leaves.

YIELD: 8 HORS D'OEUVRES

VEAL TOURNEDOS ELYSEE

8 slices white bread

2 tablespoons butter

Eight 2-ounce veal tournedos

Pinch each salt and ground white pepper

3 tablespoons vegetable oil

½ head romaine lettuce

¼ cup mayonnaise

½ cup heavy cream

Pinch each paprika and sugar

Few drops lemon juice

Salt to taste

⅔ cup Madeira Aspic, following

Using a pastry cutter, cut the bread into eight 2-inch rounds. Melt the butter in a medium sauté pan or skillet over medium heat. Add the bread rounds and fry until golden brown on both sides. Remove the bread and set aside on paper towels.

Rub the veal with salt and white pepper. Heat the oil in a sauté pan or skillet. Add the veal and sauté 6 minutes, turning once. Remove the veal and drain on paper towels.

Cut the lettuce into fine strips and place in a bowl. In a medium bowl, beat together the mayonnaise, cream, paprika, sugar, and lemon juice. Season with salt. Stir together the mayonnaise mixture and lettuce strips.

Arrange the lettuce mixture on the fried bread rounds. Top with the sautéed veal pieces. Coat the veal with Madeira Aspic. Let stand to set.

YIELD: 8 HORS D'OEUVRES

MADEIRA ASPIC

2 egg whites

1 small onion, minced

1 leek, minced

1 celery stalk, minced

1 parsley sprig

Pinch of salt

8 white peppercorns

½ bay leaf

4 cups fat-free clear meat stock

½ cup Madeira

2 envelopes (2 tablespoons) plain gelatin

Beat the egg whites until thick and frothy but not too stiff. Stir the minced vegetables into the egg whites along with the salt, pepper-corns, and bay leaf. In a large saucepan, heat the meat stock and wine. Stir in the egg white mixture. Bring to a boil over high heat, whisking vigorously to prevent the egg whites from sticking to the bottom or sides of the pan. As the egg whites rise to the surface, they will collect all the impurities in the stock. Continue to simmer the stock over very low heat for 40 to 50 minutes but do not boil.

Strain the stock carefully through a sieve lined with a double thickness of paper towel. Pour 3 tablespoons of stock into a small bowl. Stand the bowl in a saucepan of hot water. Sprinkle the gelatin over the stock. If the stock has cooled too much during filtering, heat it again before adding the gelatin, without letting it boil. Stir well; cool, stirring occasionally. Wait until the aspic is just beginning to set to use as a coating; chill leftover aspic until firm, then chop and use as a garnish for other dishes.

YIELD: ABOUT 4 CUPS

THE BIG FOUR

When the rails of the Central Pacific and Union Pacific were joined at Promontory Point, Utah, in the spring of 1869, the dreams of C.P. Huntington, Charles Crocker, Mark Hopkins, and Leland Stanford were realized. These men, who were known as the Big Four, started from behind the counters of pioneer stores in Sacramento and, in less than two decades, shouldered their way to places of national importance. They all resided in elegant mansions surrounding the present location of the Big Four restaurant on Nob Hill in San Francisco.

The Big Four held center stage in California for more than a third of a century, and the wealth of material in the Big Four restaurant attempts to capture the era when these men reigned supreme over all aspects of the Pacific Coast. Big Four chef Gloria Ciccarone prepared the following menu for a reception accompanied by the music of Cole Porter, George Gershwin, and Duke Ellington. These composers lived during the presidential administrations of Herbert Hoover and Franklin Roosevelt, and Gloria notes that "during the administrations of presidents Herbert Hoover and Franklin Roosevelt, many interesting and unusual dishes were created by White House chefs for the frequent and elegant receptions hosted by these great men."

∧ ∧ ∧ ∧ ∧

MENU

HUNTER'S TOAST

SILVER OAK CELLARS 1978 CABERNET SAUVIGNON

SWEETBREADS ON TOASTED BLACK BREAD WITH GREEN-PEPPERCORN MAYONNAISE

SONOMA CUTRER WINERY 1982 CHARDONNAY

TERRAPIN WASHINGTON

VEUVE CLICQUOT N/V BRUT

MARY RATTLEY'S VIRGINIA HAM WITH CORN MUFFINS AND CRANBERRY-ORANGE SAUCE

CHALONE VINEYARDS 1979 PINOT NOIR

HUNTER'S TOAST

6 tablespoons butter

10 *shiitake* mushrooms, thinly sliced

15 large common store mushrooms, thinly sliced

10 slices homemade bread, trimmed of crusts

Prepared hot mustard

2 tablespoons minced fresh parsley

2 pounds roast veal or smoked duck, cut into 10 slices

10 slices Emmenthal cheese

Parsley sprigs

Preheat the oven to 350°. Melt the butter in a sauté pan or skillet and sauté the mushrooms until their liquid is cooked away. Toast the bread on both sides. Cut each slice in half on the diagonal. Spread one side with a thin layer of the hot mustard and sprinkle with chopped parsley. Place a slice of roast veal or smoked duck on each slice. Arrange the sautéed mushrooms on top of the bread and cover with a slice of Emmenthal cheese. Place in the oven for 2 to 3 minutes or until the cheese is bubbly. Garnish with parsley.

YIELD: 20 HORS D'OEUVRES

SWEETBREADS ON TOASTED BLACK BREAD WITH GREEN-PEPPERCORN MAYONNAISE

2 pounds sweetbreads

Vinegar

1 small onion, sliced

2 celery stalks with leaves

2 bay leaves

20 common store mushrooms, stemmed

20 slices black bread, toasted and cut into rounds

Green-Peppercorn Mayonnaise, following

Truffle bits or minced tomato (optional)

Wash the sweetbreads in cold water, then soak in cold water for 1½ hours, changing the water several times. Place the sweetbreads in a large pot, measure out cold water to cover, and add 1 tablespoon vinegar per quart of water. Bring to a boil and simmer 3 to 5 minutes. Drain and plunge into cold water. Remove the filament and tubes. Pour enough water to cover the sweetbreads into a large pot. Add the onion, celery, and bay leaves. Bring to a boil, add the sweetbreads, and simmer covered 15 to 20 minutes. Drain the sweetbreads, let cool, and slice ¼ inch thick.

Poach the mushroom caps in boiling water for 3 to 5 minutes. Spread a thin layer of Green-Peppercorn Mayonnaise on each round of toast. Top with a slice of poached sweetbreads and a poached mushroom cap; these may be garnished with bits of truffle or a dab of minced tomato.

YIELD: 20 HORS D'OEUVRES

GREEN-PEPPERCORN MAYONNAISE

2 egg yolks

¼ to ½ teaspoon dry mustard

½ teaspoon salt

½ teaspoon distilled white vinegar or fresh lemon juice

1 teaspoon green peppercorns, crushed

½ cup olive oil

1½ tablespoons distilled white vinegar

2 tablespoons fresh lemon juice

½ cup vegetable oil

Place the egg yolks in a medium-sized bowl and beat with a whisk. Beat in the dry mustard, salt, ½ teaspoon vinegar or lemon juice, and peppercorns. Beat in the olive oil slowly, ½ teaspoon at a time. Combine the 1½ tablespoons vinegar and 2 tablespoons lemon juice. Whisk in the vegetable oil, alternating it drop by drop with a few drops of the lemon and vinegar mixture until the mixture is emulsified well.

YIELD: ABOUT 1½ CUPS

TERRAPIN WASHINGTON

This dish is very rich and is best served with a dry champagne.

1 cup *crème fraîche* (see page 123)

1 cup heavy cream

½ cup dry champagne

Leaves from 1 bunch fresh thyme, minced

¼ cup dry sherry

2 pounds canned turtle meat

Salt and ground white pepper

2 tablespoons butter

Snipped fresh chives

40 buttered toast triangles

In a heavy saucepan, cook the *crème fraîche*, heavy cream, champagne, and thyme leaves over medium heat until reduced by one-half (the sauce should coat the back of a spoon). Add the sherry and turtle meat and simmer for 10 minutes. Add salt and white pepper to taste. Whisk in the butter. Serve warm, sprinkled with chives and accompanied with buttered toast triangles.

YIELD: 40 HORS D'OEUVRES

MARY RATTLEY'S VIRGINIA HAM

Mary Rattley was President Hoover's cook. This is one of her famous hors d'oeuvres recipes.

One 11-to-14-pound Virginia or country ham

2 cups brown sugar

2 cups cider vinegar

1 cup red currant jelly

3 cups fresh white bread crumbs

Corn Muffins, following

Cranberry-Orange Sauce, following

Wash the ham and soak it for 24 hours in cold water to cover. Scrub it well. Place the ham in a large pot and add cold water to cover. Add the brown sugar and vinegar. Bring this mixture to a boil and simmer slowly until the skin of the ham puckers. Let it cool in its own water to retain the juices. Preheat the oven to 350°. Drain the ham, remove the skin, and rub the ham with currant jelly. Cover the ham with bread crumbs and brown it for 45 minutes to 1 hour.

Thinly slice the ham and serve it between small corn muffins that have been split and spread with Cranberry-Orange Sauce.

YIELD: 60 HORS D'OEUVRES

CORN MUFFINS

¾ cup sifted all-purpose flour

2½ teaspoons baking powder

1 to 2 tablespoons sugar

¾ teaspoon salt

1¼ cups yellow or white cornmeal

2 to 3 tablespoons melted butter or pan drippings from ham

1 cup milk

1 egg, beaten

Preheat the oven to 425°. Grease the muffin tins with oil or bacon drippings. Sift the dry ingredients together. Add the butter and milk to the egg. Combine the wet and dry ingredients with a few rapid strokes. Fill the muffin cups two-thirds full. Bake 20 to 25 minutes or until the muffins are lightly browned.

YIELD: ABOUT FIFTEEN 2-INCH MUFFINS

CRANBERRY-ORANGE SAUCE

1 cup water

1 cup fresh-squeezed orange juice

2 cups sugar

1 pound (4 cups) cranberries, washed and picked over

1 teaspoon grated orange zest

Place the water, orange juice, and sugar in a saucepan and stir until the sugar is dissolved. Boil the syrup 5 minutes. Add the cranberries. Gently simmer the berries in the syrup uncovered, without stirring, for 5 minutes. Add the grated orange zest. Let cool.

YIELD: ABOUT 4 CUPS

The Lodge at Pebble Beach™

Charles Crocker's Old Hotel Del Monte, which opened in 1880 as "the grandest resort hotel on the Pacific Coast," was the predecessor to The Lodge at Pebble Beach. The structure that stands today amid one of nature's most magnificent settings replaced the old hotel in 1917.

The Lodge is located in a seven-thousand-acre preserve which includes the Del Monte Forest, the world-famous 17 Mile Drive, and the Pebble Beach Golf Course. It offers spacious and tranquil accommodations and four distinguished restaurants, as well as the finest sporting facilities for golf, tennis, swimming, fishing, horseback riding, and hiking. The Lodge's Executive Chef, Franklin Biggs, created the following hors d'oeuvres recipes.

∧ ∧ ∧ ∧ ∧

MENU

SCAMPI WITH GREEN PEPPERCORNS,
GARLIC, AND SUN-DRIED TOMATOES

CHICKEN DRUMETTES WITH DIJON AND
FRESH HERBS

MARINATED MUSSELS WITH TOMATO
CONCASSE ON THE HALF-SHELL

GOLDEN AND BELUGA CAVIAR
CANAPES

SCAMPI WITH GREEN PEPPERCORNS, GARLIC, AND SUN-DRIED TOMATOES

¼ cup vegetable oil

40 jumbo shrimp (16 to 20 per pound), peeled and deveined

Cloves from 2 whole garlic bulbs, minced

¼ cup green peppercorns

1 tablespoon coarse-ground pepper

1 cup chopped fresh basil

¼ cup chopped fresh parsley

½ cup diced sun-dried tomatoes

1 cup heavy cream

4 tablespoons unsalted butter

Croutons (optional)

Parsley sprigs

Lemon slices

Heat the oil in a sauté pan or skillet. Add the shrimp and half the garlic. When the shrimp are pink in color, remove them from the pan with a slotted spoon and set aside. Add the peppercorns, remaining garlic, pepper, basil, parsley, and tomatoes to the pan. Sauté these ingredients for a few minutes before adding the cream. When the sauce has thickened, remove it from the heat and stir in the butter. Add the shrimp and serve hot. Garnish with croutons, parsley sprigs, and lemon slices.

YIELD: HORS D'OEUVRES FOR 20 PEOPLE

CHICKEN DRUMETTES WITH DIJON AND FRESH HERBS

40 chicken wings

2 cups fresh sourdough bread crumbs

3 tablespoons minced fresh parsley

2 tablespoons minced fresh rosemary

2 tablespoons minced fresh thyme

1 tablespoon coarse-ground pepper

¼ cup minced garlic

¼ cup melted butter

½ cup Dijon mustard

½ cup orange marmalade

½ cup creamed horseradish

Leaves from 1 head romaine lettuce, washed, dried, and cut into shreds

Preheat the oven to 350°. With a cleaver or large French knife, cut off the bottom portion of each wing above the joint at the end of the elbow. Scrape the meat towards the opposite end, forming a mini-drumstick. In a bowl, mix the bread crumbs, herbs, pepper, garlic, and melted butter. Dip the meat end of the drumettes in the mustard, then dredge in the herbed bread crumbs. Place on a baking sheet and bake for approximately 20 minutes, or until golden brown.

Mix the marmalade and horseradish together to make a dip. In a basket lined with a white napkin, make a bed of the shredded romaine. Serve the drumettes on the lettuce, with the dip alongside.

YIELD: 40 HORS D'OEUVRES

MARINATED MUSSELS WITH TOMATO CONCASSE ON THE HALF-SHELL

40 medium-sized mussels, scrubbed and beards removed

½ cup virgin olive oil

½ cup red wine vinegar

2 tablespoons chopped fresh oregano

1 lemon, halved

¼ cup minced garlic

Salt and pepper

Small pinch of saffron

5 tomatoes, peeled, seeded, and finely diced

20 lemon zest strips

Lime wedges

Steam the mussels until they start to open. Cool slightly, then remove them from the shell. Reserve 40 half-shells. In a nonmetal container, mix together the olive oil, vinegar, oregano, juice of ½ lemon, half of the garlic, and salt, pepper and saffron to taste. While the mussels are still warm, place them in the marinade. Cover and marinate in the refrigerator for several hours or up to 2 to 3 days.

In a sauté pan or skillet, sauté the tomatoes, the remaining garlic and lemon juice, and salt and pepper to taste over high heat until all the excess liquid has evaporated. Fill the half-shells with the tomatoes and place 1 mussel in each shell, using 2 strips of lemon zest for garnish. Serve in a bowl on a bed of crushed ice. Garnish with lime wedges.

YIELD: 40 MUSSELS

GOLDEN AND BELUGA CAVIAR
CANAPES

1 cup sour cream

1 cup liquid Aspic, following

4 ounces golden caviar

2 loaves Russian rye bread, sliced thin

1 ounce beluga caviar

40 bay shrimp

40 parsley leaves

Dill sprigs

Tomato rose (optional)

In a bowl, mix the sour cream and aspic with a wooden spoon (using a whip will create bubbles). Add the golden caviar, stirring lightly so as not to bruise or break the caviar. Let the mixture stand. When it begins to solidify, spread the mixture approximately ¼ inch thick on the bread slices. Place the bread slices on a wire rack on a baking sheet. When the mixture is totally solidified, cut the bread into diamonds or, if you have aspic cutters, cut into preferred shapes. Garnish each canapé with a dollop of beluga, a bay shrimp, and a parsley leaf. Glaze with a thin coat of aspic, if desired. Serve on a platter garnished with dill, and a tomato rose, if you like.

YIELD: 40 CANAPÉS

ASPIC

1 envelope (1 tablespoon) plain gelatin

1½ cups fish stock

2 to 3 tablespoons cognac, dry port, or Madeira

Sprinkle the gelatin over the fish stock and let soften for several minutes, then stir over low heat until all gelatin granules have dissolved completely. Remove from heat and stir in cognac or wine to taste.

YIELD: 1½ CUPS

THE GARDEN COURT

The Palace Hotel was the dream of William Ralston and William Sharon. Construction began in 1874, and on completion in 1875 it stood a grandiose seven stories high, the dining room was the largest in the west, and its carriage entrance, the Grand Court, with its paired Doric columns and opaque glass roof, housed rare tropical plants. During its first thirty-one years of existence, the hotel hosted presidents, princes, poets, generals, and the greatest stage and operatic personalities of the era. When the great earthquake struck San Francisco in 1906, only a small section of the hotel was damaged, but it was decided to raze the old Palace in October of 1906. The hotel as it stands today was completed in 1907. It is a magnificent structure that covers almost two acres in the heart of San Francisco.

The Sheraton Corporation took over the Palace Hotel in 1954 from the granddaughter of the original owner, Senator William Sharon, and has maintained the traditional luxury and elegance of the Palace. The hotel offers six hundred guest rooms and suites, private dining room suites, and five bars and restaurants. The most famous of these room is the Garden Court, which has been called "the most beautiful dining room in the world." In this room Woodrow Wilson gave his famous League of Nations speech and the United Nations held its official opening banquet. The hotel's Executive Chef, Joseph Curila, presented me with the following recipes, which include hors d'oeuvres that are both traditional and new to the Garden Court.

∧ ∧ ∧ ∧ ∧

MENU

OYSTERS KIRKPATRICK

ARTICHOKES RALSTON A LA GARDEN
COURT

CELERY VICTOR

LUMPIAS

WHARFSIDER

OYSTERS KIRKPATRICK

This dish originated in the Palace and was named for the first general manager, Col. John C. Kirkpatrick.

1 dozen very fresh oysters in their shells

KIRKPATRICK SAUCE

1 cup catsup

1 cup chili sauce

1 teaspoon Worcestershire sauce

½ teaspoon A-1 Sauce

½ small green bell pepper, minced

1 teaspoon chopped fresh parsley

4 bacon slices, each cut in 3 pieces

Rock salt

½ cup freshly grated Parmesan cheese

Preheat the oven to 350°. Shuck the oysters and place each one in its rounded half shell. Mix together all the sauce ingredients and set aside. Blanch the bacon for 5 minutes, remove from the pan with a slotted spoon, and drain on paper towels.

Place the oysters on a bed of rock salt. Cover each oyster with the sauce. Sprinkle with the cheese, and top with a piece of bacon. Bake for 12 minutes.

YIELD: 12 OYSTERS

ARTICHOKES RALSTON
A LA GARDEN COURT

The recipe for Artichokes Ralston was created by Chef Philip Roemer and named after the founder of the Palace Hotel, William C. Ralston.

12 large artichokes

2 lemons, cut in half

1 cup distilled white vinegar

FILLING

1 tablespoon chopped shallot

2 tablespoons butter

¾ pound common store mushrooms, minced (about 3 cups)

1 tablespoon fresh lemon juice

½ cup chopped ham

½ cup Brown Sauce (see page 195)

½ cup white bread crumbs

Salt

Diced and buttered mixed vegetables

Mornay Sauce, following

12 Oysters Kirkpatrick, preceding

Bordelaise Sauce, following

Cut off the base of the artichokes and break off all the leaves up to the top third; cut off the top with a sharp knife. Trim off all the green

continued

and cut out the choke. Rub all over with a cut lemon. Add the vinegar to a large pot of boiling salted water and cook the artichokes until tender, about 30 minutes.

Preheat the oven to 350°. To make the filling, in a sauté pan or skillet, sauté the shallot in the butter until translucent. Add the mushrooms and lemon juice and cook until all the liquid is evaporated. Add the ham, brown sauce, and bread crumbs and cook until thickened; stir frequently. Remove from the heat and add salt to taste.

Fill 6 artichoke hearts with the mushroom filling. Fill the remaining artichoke hearts with your favorite combination of diced and buttered mixed vegetables and top with Mornay sauce. Place the hearts in a buttered shallow pan and bake until the tops are brown (about 20 minutes).

Meanwhile, prepare 12 Oysters Kirkpatrick. Place the artichokes and oysters on a serving dish and top the mushroom-filled artichoke hearts with bordelaise sauce. Serve very hot on cocktail plates.

YIELD: 24 HORS D'OEUVRES

MORNAY SAUCE

3 tablespoons butter

3 tablespoons flour

1¼ cups liquid (milk or chicken, fish, or vegetable broth), warmed

Salt and pepper to taste

Ground nutmeg to taste

½ cup freshly grated Parmesan or Swiss cheese

Melt the butter in a saucepan. Add the flour and cook over low heat 2 to 3 minutes, stirring gently. Gradually stir in the liquid and continue to stir until mixture thickens. Season to taste, add the cheese, and blend thoroughly.

YIELD: ABOUT 2 CUPS

BORDELAISE SAUCE

2 tablespoons chopped green onions

½ cup dry red wine

½ tablespoon chopped fresh parsley

1 cup Brown Sauce (see page 195)

4 medium-sized beef marrow bones, split in half

1 cup water

Salt

½ tablespoon butter

Place the onions, wine, and parsley in a saucepan over medium heat and reduce this mixture to one-fourth its volume. Add the brown sauce and simmer 10 minutes. Meanwhile, remove the marrow from the bones and dice. Bring the water to a boil in a medium saucepan; add salt to taste. Cook 2 cups of the diced marrow in the water for 1 minute and then drain. Add the marrow to the sauce and stir in the butter.

YIELD: 1 CUP

CELERY VICTOR

This now-famous appetizer was created by Chef Philip Roemer at the Palace Hotel in the early twenties.

4 celery stalks

MARINADE

2 cups water

½ cup vinegar

½ cup oil

Juice of 2 lemons

2 bay leaves, 1 parsley sprig, 1 thyme sprig, and 1 teaspoon
peppercorns tied in a cheesecloth bag

Lettuce leaves

½ cup cooked shrimp or crab meat

2 chopped hard-cooked eggs

5 anchovy fillets

Sliced tomatoes

Cut the lower third of each celery stalk lengthwise into 3 sections; place them in a saucepan. Mix together the marinade ingredients. Pour the marinade over the celery and simmer until tender. Cool the celery in the marinade. Drain. Put the celery on a bed of lettuce leaves and cover with the shrimp, chopped eggs, and anchovies. Garnish with sliced tomatoes.

YIELD: 12 HORS D'OEUVRES

LUMPIAS

1 cup minced green onions

4 garlic cloves, minced

2 tablespoons peanut oil

1 cup shredded white cabbage

½ cup chopped green beans

One double chicken breast, cooked, skinned, boned, and shredded

1 cup shredded cooked pork

1 cup shredded cooked prawns

½ cup bean sprouts

Salt and pepper to taste

2 tablespoons light soy sauce

1 package egg roll wrappers

Oil for deep-frying

Lumpia Sauce, following

In a large sauté pan or skillet, sauté the onions and garlic in the peanut oil until they are translucent. Add the cabbage and beans and sauté until tender. Add the chicken, pork, prawns, and bean sprouts and season with salt, pepper, and soy sauce. Sauté until heated through.

Place 1 tablespoon of the filling mixture in the center of an egg roll wrapper. Fold in the edges of the wrapper and roll. Continue this process until all of the filling is used. Heat oil to 350°, drop in the *lumpias*, and fry until golden. Drain on paper towels and serve with the *lumpia* sauce.

YIELD: ABOUT 24 HORS D'OEUVRES

LUMPIA SAUCE

4 tablespoons sugar

¼ cup light soy sauce

1 cup chicken broth or water

2 tablespoons cornstarch mixed with ¼ cup cold water

1 garlic clove crushed with ¼ teaspoon salt

Combine the sugar, soy sauce, and broth in a saucepan. Bring to a boil. Add the cornstarch mixture smoothly and stir until the mixture thickens. Simmer, stirring for 1 minute. Stir in the garlic crushed with salt.

YIELD: 1¼ CUPS

WHARFSIDER

3 ounces common store mushrooms, sliced

6 tablespoons butter

1¼ cups cooked fresh crab meat

1¼ cups cooked bay shrimp

1/4 cup Béchamel Sauce, following

6 slices white bread, trimmed of crusts, toasted, and cut in half on the diagonal

1 cup Hollandaise Sauce, page 180

Preheat the broiler. In a sauté pan or skillet, sauté the mushrooms in the butter for 2 minutes, then add the crab and the shrimp and cook for 1 minute or until thoroughly warm. Remove from the heat and fold the béchamel sauce into this mixture.

Place the toasted bread on a flat baking sheet and equally divide the seafood and mushroom mixture among the slices, spreading the mixture evenly on each slice. Cover each portion with hollandaise sauce and quickly put them under the broiler until evenly browned. Serve on small cocktail plates.

YIELD: 12 HORS D'OEUVRES

BECHAMEL SAUCE

1 tablespoon butter

1½ tablespoons flour

1 cup hot milk

Salt to taste

Melt the butter in a heavy saucepan and stir in the flour until bubbly. Whisk in the milk until blended. Cook and whisk over medium heat until thickened. Season to taste.

YIELD: ABOUT 1 CUP

HOLLANDAISE SAUCE

3 egg yolks

2 tablespoons fresh lemon juice

1 cup (2 sticks) melted butter

Salt and pepper to taste

Place the egg yolks in a blender and add the lemon juice. Blend the egg yolks and, with the motor running, pour in ½ cup melted butter in a very thin stream; the yolks will emulsify to a thick sauce. Remove the sauce from the blender and slowly whisk in the remaining ½ cup melted butter. Season and keep warm over very low heat.

Yield: 1½ cups

STANFORD COURT

The Stanford Court is a luxury hotel built on the site of the famed Leland Stanford mansion on San Francisco's Nob Hill. Stanford—railroad magnate, United States senator, governor of California, and founder of Stanford University— completed his mansion in 1876, but in 1906 it went up in flames during the devastating earthquake that wiped out most of San Francisco. A new building, the Stanford Court apartments, opened in 1913 and was later remodeled to create the hotel as it is today.

Jim Nassikas, creator of the Stanford Court Hotel, and its president and managing partner, is a perfectionist and looks back on eleven consecutive Mobil 5-Star Awards and the Diplome de l'Excellence Européenne. These recipes for *Menus and Music* were created at the Stanford Court by Executive Chef de Cuisine Christian Iser, who is in charge of the varied food service operations of the hotel as well as the hotel's award-winning Fournou's Ovens restaurant.

∧   ∧   ∧   ∧   ∧

MENU

GOLDEN CAVIAR AND NEW POTATOES

MAINE LOBSTER BRIOCHE

SMOKED STURGEON MOUSSE WITH
BELGIAN ENDIVE

SERRANO-PEPPERED GUACAMOLE WITH
MONTEREY JACK

VINEYARD SNAILS IN CLAY POTS

GOLDEN CAVIAR AND NEW POTATOES

12 to 14 very small red potatoes (1 pound or less)

4 to 5 cups rock salt

Oil for deep-frying

About ½ cup sour cream

One 14-ounce tin fresh caviar or less

Preheat the oven to 450°. Wash and dry the potatoes. Arrange them on a bed of rock salt and place in the oven. Bake for 30 to 35 minutes or until tender. Remove the potatoes and slice them in half. Scoop out the center pulp with a melon-ball cutter or small spoon and reserve both the pulp and skins. Mash the pulp slightly and keep it warm.

Heat the oil for deep-frying to 375°. Drop the potato shells into the oil and cook quickly until golden brown and crisp. Remove with a slotted spoon and drain well on paper towels.

Fill the shells with the mashed potato mixture. Top each with a spoonful or so of sour cream. Then add a teaspoon or more of caviar to the top. Serve on a bed of the hot rock salt, if desired.

YIELD: 24 TO 28 HORS D'OEUVRES

MAINE LOBSTER BRIOCHE

1 cup small-diced cooked lobster meat (from approximately a 1¼-
   pound lobster)

⅓ cup small-diced baby beans, blanched and chilled

⅓ cup small-diced seeded and peeled tomatoes

⅓ to ½ cup homemade mayonnaise

2 tablespoons chopped fresh tarragon

Salt and fresh-ground black pepper to taste

Fifteen ½-inch-thick slices *brioche*

2 tablespoons chopped fresh parsley

Prepare a salad by mixing together the lobster, beans, tomatoes, mayonnaise, and tarragon. Season with salt and pepper.

Toast each slice of brioche until golden and then cut out into 2½ or 3-inch-by-1¾-inch ovals. Spread an even layer of the lobster salad ½ inch thick on the ovals. Sprinkle with parsley and serve.

YIELD: 12 TO 15 SLICES

SMOKED STURGEON MOUSSE WITH BELGIAN ENDIVE

4 ounces cream cheese

6 ounces smoked sturgeon

White pepper

12 endive leaves, each about 3 inches long

1 ounce domestic black caviar

1 chive, minced

Combine the cream cheese and smoked sturgeon in a blender or food processor. Do not add any salt since the smoked sturgeon is already salty enough. Add white pepper to taste.

Put the mousse into a pastry bag. Pipe the mousse onto each endive leaf and top with a few eggs of caviar and a few pieces of the chopped chive.

YIELD: 12 HORS D'OEUVRES

SERRANO-PEPPERED GUACAMOLE WITH MONTEREY JACK

Two 8-inch or three 6-inch corn tortillas

Oil for deep-frying

2 thin slices Monterey jack, each about 8 inches square

1 ripe avocado

Fresh lime juice to taste

Minced onion to taste

Minced cilantro to taste

1 *serrano* pepper, seeded and minced

Salt and pepper

2 pitted black olives

Cilantro leaves

Using a 1½-inch plain round cutter, cut out 12 tortilla chips. In a heavy sauté pan or skillet, pour the oil to a depth of ½ inch. Heat the oil to almost smoking. Fry the chips until they are golden brown. Remove from the pan with a slotted spoon and drain on paper towels. Using the same cutter, cut 12 cheese chips to go on top of each tortilla. Arrange the tortillas with cheese on an ovenproof platter.

To make the guacamole, use a fork to mash the avocado together with the lime juice, onion, cilantro, and *serrano* pepper. Salt and pepper to taste. Before serving, heat the tortilla chips in a 350° oven until the cheese just begins to melt. Scrape the guacamole into a bag with a decorative tube and pipe out the guacamole on each tortilla chip. Cut the black olives in sections (8 per olive) and place on top of the guacamole. Garnish with cilantro leaves.

YIELD: 12 HORS D'OEUVRES

VINEYARD SNAILS IN CLAY POTS

1½ cups (3 sticks) plus 2 tablespoons soft unsalted butter

3 tablespoons minced shallots

4 garlic cloves, minced

6 hazelnuts, peeled and minced

36 canned vineyard snails

Rock salt

Preheat oven to 375°. Mix all of the ingredients, except the snails and salt, and whip to a cream. Place 6 snails in each of 6 small clay pots (1¾ inches in diameter and 1½ inches high) and then stuff each pot generously with the butter. Fill a metal dish with rock salt and arrange the 6 snail pots so that they are partially immersed in the salt. Bake about 12 minutes.

Variation: Cover each snail pot with a cap of puff pastry and bake until golden brown.

YIELD: 6 SERVINGS

THE WESTIN ST. FRANCIS
San Francisco

At the turn of the century, the San Francisco city fathers realized the importance of Union Square as a focal point of the city. They landscaped the park and added a monument commemorating Admiral Dewey's victory at Manila Bay. A group of enterprising businessmen full of civic pride formed the San Francisco Hotel Company and decided to open a luxury hotel facing the park. After making an extensive study of all the important European hotels, they went ahead with a stately two-wing twelve-story design that opened to the public as the St. Francis Hotel in 1904. The great fire following the earthquake of 1906 damaged the original St. Francis, but the structural repairs needed were minimal and restoration was primarily devoted to refinishing the interior. In November 1907, the restored St. Francis was reopened with two wings fully completed of a new three-wing hotel design. A fourth wing was opened in 1913, making the St. Francis the largest hotel on the Pacific Coast. Over the years the hotel has welcomed guests of international prominence including royalty, politicians, military dignitaries, theatrical luminaries, and the literati.

In 1954, the St. Francis joined the family of Westin Hotels, and in 1972 a thirty-two-story tower was added, which brought the room capacity to twelve hundred, increased convention and meeting space, and added a Grand Ballroom which accommodates fifteen hundred for receptions. The final restoration of the main building was competed in 1983 in time for the stay of Queen Elizabeth II and President Reagan at the hotel.

∧ ∧ ∧ ∧ ∧

MENU

CHERRY TOMATOES STUFFED WITH A
PANACHE OF MARINATED VEGETABLES

MADRAS
ORANGE BLOSSOM

ESCARGOTS AND SWEETBREADS IN
BOUCHEE SHELLS

MIDNIGHT SUN
ITALIAN FLAME

CHICKEN BROCHETTE WITH LYCHEES

DUBONNET COCKTAIL
VERMOUTH COCKTAIL

LOBSTER MEDALLIONS WITH CAVIAR
AND DILL

KIR ROYALE
L'AIGLON

PEARS WITH ROQUEFORT AND PECANS

MIDORI SUNSHINE
PEACH TANG

CHERRY TOMATOES
STUFFED WITH A PANACHE
OF MARINATED VEGETABLES

2 tablespoons olive oil

1 small carrot, zucchini, yellow squash, and red bell pepper, each
   cut into very small cubes

½ cup rice wine vinegar or distilled white vinegar

Salt and pepper to taste

20 firm ripe cherry tomatoes

Heat the olive oil in a saucepan. Add the carrot, zucchini, squash
and pepper and sauté for 30 seconds. Add the vinegar, salt, and
pepper and simmer for 1 minute. Remove and let cool. Cut the tops
off the tomatoes and remove the seeds. Stuff the tomatoes with the
vegetables.

YIELD: 20 HORS D'OEUVRES

MADRAS

1¼ ounces vodka

2 ounces cranberry juice

2 ounces fresh orange juice

2 cranberries

Place a few ice cubes in a highball glass. Pour in the vodka, cranberry juice, and orange juice and float 2 cranberries on top.

YIELD: 1 DRINK

ORANGE BLOSSOM

1¼ ounces gin

2 ounces freshly squeezed orange juice

1 tablespoon simple syrup*

Orange slice

Stir the gin, orange juice, and simple syrup with ice and then strain into a martini glass. Garnish with the orange slice.

YIELD: 1 DRINK

* To make simple syrup, boil 2 parts sugar to 1 part water for 5 minutes in a heavy pan. Store in the refrigerator.

ESCARGOTS AND SWEETBREADS IN BOUCHEE SHELLS

2 shallots, chopped

2 tablespoons butter

2 tablespoons brandy

¼ cup Madeira wine

⅔ cup heavy cream

½ cup Brown Sauce, following

Salt and pepper to taste

½ cup chopped canned escargots

½ cup chopped cooked sweetbreads (see page 155)

20 small baked puff pastry shells

Chopped fresh chives

Preheat the oven to 400°. In a sauté pan or skillet, sauté the shallots in the butter, being careful not to brown them. Deglaze the pan with the brandy and Madeira and reduce slightly. Add the cream and reduce again. Add the brown sauce, heat through, and season with salt and pepper. Add the escargots and sweetbreads and cook for 5 to 8 minutes more; check the seasoning. Heat the puff pastry shells in the oven for 5 minutes. Remove from the oven and fill the shells, using a spoon. Serve with a sprinkling of chives.

YIELD: 20 HORS D'OEUVRES

BROWN SAUCE

1½ cups low-sodium canned beef broth

½ small onion, minced

½ carrot, minced

1 parsley sprig

1 small bay leaf

1 thyme sprig

¼ cup dry white wine

1 tablespoon cornstarch mixed with 1 tablespoon water

Salt and pepper to taste

¼ cup dry sherry

In a medium saucepan, simmer the broth, vegetables, herbs, and wine together for 25 minutes. Whisk in the cornstarch mixture and simmer until thickened. Season to taste. Add the sherry and simmer a few minutes more.

YIELD: ABOUT 2 CUPS

MIDNIGHT SUN

1¼ ounces Dry Sack sherry

½ ounce Dubonnet Rouge

Thin strip of lime zest

Stir the sherry and Dubonnet with ice and then strain into a sherry glass. Garnish with the lime zest.

YIELD: 1 DRINK

ITALIAN FLAME

1¼ ounces Campari

½ ounce vodka

Thin strip lemon zest

Place a few ice cubes in a highball glass. Pour the Campari and vodka over the ice and garnish with the lemon zest.

YIELD: 1 DRINK

CHICKEN BROCHETTE WITH LYCHEES

MARINADE

1 cup soy sauce

¾ cup dry sherry

1 tablespoon sugar

¼ cup fresh lemon juice

2 tablespoons chopped fresh ginger

2 tablespoons chopped fresh cilantro

2 pounds chicken breasts, skinned and boned

20 canned lychees, cut in half*

2 green onions, cut into ½-inch pieces

Place all the ingredients for the marinade in a blender or food processor and purée. Place the marinade in a large glass or stainless steel bowl. Cut the chicken breasts into bite-sized cubes and marinate them for 3 hours in the refrigerator.

Arrange 3 cubes of chicken, 2 pieces of lychee, and 2 pieces of green onion on each of 20 skewers. Sauté or grill for 5 minutes.

YIELD: 20 HORS D'OEUVRES

* Lychees may be found in Asian food stores and many large supermarkets.

DUBONNET COCKTAIL

1 ounce gin

1 ounce Dubonnet Rouge

Thin strip of lemon zest

Stir the gin and the Dubonnet with ice and then strain into a martini glass. Garnish with the lemon zest.

YIELD: 1 DRINK

VERMOUTH COCKTAIL

5 ounces chilled chardonnay

1 ounce sweet vermouth

One thin green onion

Pour the chardonnay over the vermouth in a highball glass. Garnish with the onion.

YIELD: 1 DRINK

LOBSTER MEDALLIONS WITH CAVIAR AND DILL

COURT BOUILLON

1 small celery stalk

1 small carrot

½ small onion

3 bay leaves

Two 2-pound fresh New England or rock lobsters

7 slices rye bread

½ cup (1 stick) unsalted butter

Chopped fresh dill to taste

1 to 1½ ounces caviar

Dill sprigs

To make the court bouillon, boil the celery, carrot, onion, and bay leaves in just enough water to cover the lobster. Put the lobster into the water and cook for approximately 12 to 14 minutes. Remove the lobster and plunge it into cold water. Break the lobster apart carefully and slice the meat into medallions.

With a biscuit cutter, cut rounds of rye bread so that they are slightly smaller than the lobster medallions. Whip the butter and add the chopped dill to it. Spread the butter on the bread. Place a lobster medallion on top of each piece of bread and garnish with the caviar and a sprig of dill.

YIELD: ABOUT 20 HORS D'OEUVRES

KIR ROYALE

6 ounces champagne

½ ounce *crème de cassis*

Thin strip of orange zest

Pour the *crème de cassis* into a tulip-shaped champagne glass and then add the champagne. Garnish with the orange zest.

YIELD: 1 DRINK

L'AIGLON

6 ounces champagne

½ ounce Mandarine Napoleon

Thin strip mandarin orange zest

Pour the Mandarine Napoleon into a tulip-shaped champagne glass and then add the champagne. Garnish with the strip of mandarin orange zest.

YIELD: 1 DRINK

PEARS WITH ROQUEFORT AND PECANS

4 pears, peeled

1 lemon

4 ounces Roquefort cheese

About 6 ounces cream cheese

16 pecan halves

Cut the pears lengthwise into 4 pieces. Remove the cores. Rub some lemon juice on the fruit so that it does not change color. Mix the Roquefort and cream cheese together in a mixing bowl. Scrape this mixture into a piping bag with a star tube and pipe onto the pear. Garnish with the pecans.

YIELD: 16 PIECES

MIDORI SUNSHINE

5 ounces freshly squeezed orange juice

1¼ ounces Midori

Cantaloupe wedge

Place a few ice cubes in a glass. Pour the orange juice and Midori over the ice and garnish with a cantaloupe wedge.

YIELD: 1 DRINK

PEACH TANG

5 ounces freshly squeezed grapefruit juice

1¼ ounces peach schnapps

Fresh peach slice

Place a few ice cubes in a glass. Pour the grapefruit juice and peach schnapps over the ice and garnish with a peach slice.

YIELD: 1 DRINK

INDEX

SHARON O'CONNOR is the author and publisher of the *Menus and Music* series. She is the cellist and founder of the San Francisco String Quartet and has been performing with the quartet for more than ten years. She founded the Classic Jazz Septet in 1986.